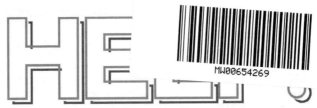

MY GAMES STINK

52 AMAZING GAMES FOR YOUTH MINISTRY

JON FORREST

randall house

JOHNSON
UNIVERSITY
FLORIDA
LIBRARY

© 2017 by Jon Forrest

Published by Randall House Publications
114 Bush Road
Nashville, TN 37217

All rights reserved. No part of this publication may be reproduced, stored in a retrieval system, or transmitted in any form or by any means—electronic, mechanical, photocopy, recording, or any other means—except for brief quotation in critical reviews, without the prior permission of the publisher.

Printed in the United States of America

13-ISBN 9780892659968

**For Carrie and Ellie...
and for Mom and Dad too
in case this is my last book.**

Table of Contents

Introduction

Punctuation is incredibly important in the title of this book. When you were learning about commas in the fifth grade, your teacher probably illustrated this by showing you the sentence where punctuation could save your grandpa's life.

There is a huge difference between, "Let's eat Grandpa" and "Let's eat, Grandpa." That little comma means everything to Grandpa.

Punctuation is vital to the name of this book as well. I do not want to help you stink up your games. Until a few years ago, game stinking was my specialty. There is such a fine line between a great icebreaker and a boring lullaby of unconsciousness.

So, to keep your game time the best it can be, remember the following points as you plan and prep. This is the crazy important stuff!

1. Be energetic and sold out to whichever game you're leading. It's all about the experience.
2. People should be having fun before they even know they are playing a game. Do NOT explain the fun out of everything (like I am doing now.) They will learn as they play.
3. Interesting prizes save weak games.
4. Stop while people are still having fun.

Up-front Credits

Some of the games in the following pages are original, born in my tumultuous mind. But, many of the entries come from seeds of games I have seen played at camps, gatherings, or other student ministry meetings.

I want to give credit to people wherever I can. However, it's impossible to trace most games we play back to their source. Some of these games have been around a long time and have morphed over the years. You probably played them when you were younger.

Probably the best way to describe this book is to call it a collection of fun games I have discovered in my ministry. I hope you enjoy them as well!

I also want to say, "Thank you, Mr. Gorilla-Man-Gun Creator— whoever you are. I wish I could find you to shake your hand and get permission to share your awesome game, but until that day I hope you don't mind if I teach some friends how to play it more effectively."

Jon Forrest

Section 1

Why Do We Need Games in the First Place?

Engagement Is Key

I heard about the pastor of a small group who scheduled a family style lock-in. He chose to have his devotion time around midnight in a stuffy room with terrible air conditioning.

One of the young boys who, more than likely, had not been engaged by the group, slipped to the back of the room and sat in a window they had opened to get a little airflow. It's hard to say whether he sat there for the fresh air or to see the more interesting activities going on outside the window.

The cool air paired with the long-winded speaker and the fact that the boy had not become involved with the service, eventually got the best of him. This was way more than nodding off. This was slobber-inducing hibernation sleep.

Regrettably, in his sleep, the boy fell out of the window. It would have been comical if it hadn't been a third-floor window. The boy died from a lack of engagement. And you thought that hole in the wall from your last lock-in was bad.

Fortunately, the pastor was the apostle Paul. He went down and raised Eutychus from the dead (Acts 20:7-12). If you can raise the dead, engaging students is not that important.

Maybe I'm being a little tough on Paul. Can you imagine how engaging he was? With that Road to Damascus story, he probably didn't need Mental Ping Pong to get kids' attention. But as I read this account from Acts, it's apparent that even Paul had students who were difficult to incorporate into group time conversation.

Finding those points of engagement is what this book is for. I hope you can use the ideas in this book to involve students who are more comfortable spectating than participating.

Teaching Students Is Like Feeding Bears in Captivity

If people were data recorders we would not need this book. Imagine being able to hit a red record button in student's brains and then just fill them with information. I'm about to make up a stat here. Students only absorb every nineteenth word you say. You can help this a little by mixing in the words "hanky-panky," "fleek," and "IMAX®."

Students are suffering from information over-saturation. It reminds me of a time when I was a kid and went to Pigeon Forge on vacation with my family. The Smoky Mountains were our vacation spot. We would always drive through the countryside hoping to see a bear. Other than the occasional hay bale my imagination turned into a bear, we never had any luck spotting one. So, you can imagine my excitement when I saw the souvenir shop that advertised "Come Feed the Live Black Bears."

I begged dad until he took me. Near the bear's huge concrete pit, we bought a third of a loaf of bread to feed this awesome creature. I was so excited until I looked down into the quarry and saw a bear that looked like he might explode if he ate one more slice of bread! The floor of this sad structure was littered with stale bread that countless kids before had tried tempting the bear's appetite without success. The disappointed kid next to me threw a slice of bread that landed on the poor creature's back; he didn't even acknowledge it.

That reminds me of our students. Can you begin to fathom the amount of information they are bombarded with? Even content they love is swiped upwards or sideways in less than a second. How in the world can we be sure they hear the only message that counts? That is not an exaggeration either. Compared to the gospel, everything else is rubbish.

Priming Students to Learn

Students must be primed for this message of life. My lesson in priming was incredibly frustrating. I wanted to make a duck race game. So, I bought two cast iron water pumps like Laura Ingalls might use. They were so cool! I mounted the pumps on fifty-five gallon drums and ran gutters away from the pumps for eight feet, and then curved them to bring the water back toward the pump where it emptied into the drum. So, when a rubber duck was put in the gutter in front of the spout and I started pumping, it would race through the gutter and end up back in front of me. At least that was the plan.

I built the whole set. I put a duck in place and started pumping the handle like a wild man. Nothing happened. I pumped harder and still nothing. I took the pump back off of the barrel and as I stuffed it back in the box I noticed the instructions. The little paper said "cebar la bomba antes de su uso." When I turned it over to the English side of the instructions it said, "Pump must be primed before use." I poured a little water down into the pump and began pumping the handle and out flowed a rolling river that merrily floated my little duck on his way.

Students are a lot like that. The priming process of playing a game does a few things. Students are much more likely to become engaged in the conversation if they are enjoying themselves. It relaxes them. You will have an easier time connecting with them if they like you as well as the person sitting next to them in a group.

My Checkered Past With Games

For years, I was on a quest to find the perfect student ministry game. I knew it was out there! I visualized myself introducing it to a room of students who would look at me as if I were this generation's Bob Barker. You know, I'd kind of have the personality of Ryan Seacrest with the prizes of Oprah on one of her give-away shows, along with the demeanor of Santa Claus.

But the truth is—there is no magic, foolproof icebreaker that will make your students have a blast, prepare them to learn, and love you. It's like a "fun exercise" or a "delicious healthy snack." They exist only in our wildest dreams.

You can, however, become a consistently good game leader when you realize a few simple tips, quit relying on the game, and focus on the experience.

All of us have heard about an incredible game from a friend, which we quickly plop out in front of our students saying, "This is fun!" only to have them pelt us with rotten vegetables.

Relying on the quality of a game to engage students is like buying a beautiful cut of steak only to bring it home and sling it in the microwave. (You may notice many of my illustrations involve eating.) You're only halfway there when you leave the butcher, or when you have an incredible game in mind.

The Subtle Shift That Can Change Everything

I wish I knew exactly how many game books I've purchased in my life. It would also be embarrassing to know how many youth ministry game videos I have watched online. I'm haunted in thinking there is a great idea out there that I haven't heard about. But there is a big problem with these resources, which is what led me to write this book. We completely explain the fun out of our games.

Here's the solution! It's the subtle shift that could change everything about your icebreaking fun time. **Game instructions are for you as the leader, not for the participants.**

You can explain what you want to do for five minutes and still have people in the dark, or you can strategically show them what you want in a simple moment and have immediate fun.

Think about it, when you go to an arcade and swipe your card to play a game, how many directions are you given? Of course, you die a time or two getting the hang of it, but in no time, you're a pro.

I fully believe most of the fun our icebreakers and games produce dies in the introduction and explanation phase. We can fix that.

In this book, you will find instructions for each game, but those instructions are just so *you* will understand the game. You will also find an example of exactly what you could say in introducing each game. There's nothing magical about the words I'll give you to say. It's more about keeping you from saying too much.

By the way, the titles that are provided are only there to help give you a reference point. Don't even bring them up to the students. They should be having fun before they even know you are playing a game.

Primum Non Nocere

This may be the least fun and most important section in this book.

Doctors have a promise in the Hippocratic oath that youth workers need to pay special attention to. They say, "*primum non nocere.*" It means "first, do no harm." Youth pastors should totally take this same oath.

Student and worker protection is so incredibly vital. I'm not sure it's our most important job, but it is our first job. I can prove it to you. Imagine that you go on this incredible mission trip every year where ten thousand people are won to Christ and every kid becomes a missionary. It's a pretty successful trip. But now imagine you lose a student in that country every 10 years when you visit. If that were the case, this otherwise ridiculously successful trip would cease to exist. You can't sidestep safety. That's why I say it is our first concern.

Keeping kids safe is important. You must repeat this phrase to yourself from time to time. "Don't do anything dumb. Don't do anything dumb." The reason you should remind yourself of this is because dumb things seem fun and look really cool in pictures and your students are drawn to them like Vanilla Ice to a reality TV show.

For instance, fifteen years ago we all played "Sardines" at a lock-in. If you are not familiar with this game, it's basically reverse hide and go seek. One person hides in the darkened church and everyone tries to find the person and hide with them. So, in about 15 minutes everyone is stuffed in the mop closet that smells like a dead mouse. Only now it also smells like fourteen pairs of teen boy's shoes with a touch of Axe Body Spray and a dead mouse. It's more fun than it sounds. Students go crazy for it.

What could possibly go wrong at the beginning of this game when there are two people locked in a dark closet? I can hear somebody say, "Well, we would send one of our workers to hide so it wouldn't be two students." That may be even worse. I hope you have instilled in your workers the wild importance of having two-deep leadership. Never be alone with a student. Even in a counseling situation be in a highly visible area with people nearby. Gender doesn't matter. You must be above reproach.

Back to our game, let's say you figured out a way not to have two people alone in the hiding place, you still have to deal with the three couples you have who could not care less about the game, but instead would find their own dark corner of the church to...how shall I say this gently, "discuss the seventh commandment."

Sardines is so much fun. And we will never play it again. Yes, I'm old. Yes, I'm really careful. But decisions like this are the reason I have been able to work with students in one place for over twenty years.

Don't misunderstand, I love dumb stuff. It's a constant struggle for me. I want to play Chubby Bunny just like you do. This is the game where students stuff marshmallows in their mouth and see how many they can get shoved in there and still be able to say, "Chubby Bunny" before they either choke to death or vomit all over the youth room. Doesn't that description make you want to play this old favorite?

People die playing this. I've seen people choke playing it. It's not a good idea. If you have a bunch of marshmallows laying around and you need a game, see who can catch one in their mouth from the farthest distance, but don't take a chance when it comes to safety.

Remember, *primum non nocere,* or in other words "don't do anything dumb!"

Section 2

No Prep/
No Props

Uh or Um

This game is piece of cake. Give a student a subject to talk about. He has to talk about it for thirty seconds without pausing or saying "uh," "um," or hesitating for 3 seconds. I'll give you a few subjects as examples, but you will probably want your kid to talk about whatever topic you're going to cover that night.

It's amazing how many kids start with, "Ummm." Remember they cannot pause or say "uh," "um," or hesitate for more than three seconds."

Buzz them with an annoying "AAAHHHH" if they mess up or delay.

Possible topics:

- Vacuum cleaners
- Pesky nose hair
- Mosquitos
- The church parking lot
- Turkey sandwiches
- The monkey cage at the zoo
- Your favorite chair
- Belly button lint
- Pets
- Pimento cheese sandwiches
- Pizza
- Cartoon characters

Say this

Darrell, how would you like to earn this delectable beef jerky? Step up here to the front of the class.

Talk about vacuum cleaners for thirty seconds without saying "uh," "um," or hesitating and you will know the joy of the jerky. Ready? GO!

Noisy room that needs quieted?
Say, "If you can hear me clap once. If you can
hear me clap twice..." By the time you get to
four claps, you could quiet the Super Dome.

2 Look Up

This is a simple game that works great with up to about fifteen people. You can play it with any number, but if you have a huge crowd it can take a little longer to complete (which is not necessarily a bad thing.)

Stand in a circle. Say, "Pick some toes." Make a witty comment about how gross that statement sounds. Explain that you are actually telling everyone to look down at someone's feet. They really need to lock in on one person's feet and not let their eyes wander. When you say, "Look up!" everyone should move their eyes up directly to the eyes of the person whose feet they were looking at.

If the two people are not looking at one another, nothing happens. If they are looking at one another they are both out. They should have a seat and the game continues. Keep playing until you have a winner.

Obviously, if you have an odd number of contestants you'll have a winner. If you have an even number you can have them play rock, paper, scissors to find a champ. Or you could just put a Mars Bar across the room and say, "First person to grab the Mars Bar is the champ."

Say this

Let's all stand in a circle. No, come on guys, that's a parallelogram you've made. Let's make a good circle.

Okay everyone look down and pick some toes. Wait, let me rephrase that. Choose some toes to look at. In just a second I will say, "Look up." When I do, I want you to quickly move your eyes from those toes you're looking at to the eyes of the person you have chosen.

If he or she is looking at your eyes, you are both out. No cheating. You can't change your gaze if the person is looking at you. And you have to look into the eyes of someone.

Okay, pick some toes. (Pause) Look up! That was just practice, but next time is for real. Winner gets to sit in any chair he or she chooses and eat a Mars® Bar while we all watch.

Buy this book for one of your volunteers. Put a little gift card in the back of it and tell her she can't have the card until she reads to that page. Challenge her to do the same thing for 200,000 of her friends.

3

Count Phalanges

No, this is not a creepy guy from Transylvania. Phalanges are fingers. This is the exciting, intense game of finger counting. Okay, I know it's not going to make the X-Games, but don't knock it until you try it.

Two people face one another. They put their hands behind their backs. While their hands are back there they choose a number between 1–10 by holding out that many fingers.

When you say "Ready? Go!" both people quickly bring their hands around to the front and the first person to add up all the fingers and say the answer wins.

If one of the contestants has any delay in bringing his hands around, he is disqualified and very possibly shunned from the group.

The winner finds a new partner and the game continues until one rules them all.

If you think math is hard, I want you to say "Math is hard" in a whiny voice.

Wow! That was incredibly whiny. Math can also be fun.

Jordin and Tosha, come up here for a minute. Face one another and put your hands behind your back. Hold up whatever number of fingers you'd like on your hands. When I say "Go" I want you to bring your hands around to the front really fast. The first person to add up all the fingers and say that number out loud is exempt from math homework for the rest of his or her life. Well, I can't guarantee that, but you get a Snickers plus a Reese's Cup and you know what that equals: happiness.

Bring those hands around fast or you are disqualified. You guys are lucky. Back in the 1800's when they played this game they would cut people's fingers off if they cheated with slow hands. We just make you sit down.

Here we go, Jordan and Tosha. Ready? Go!

Everybody find a partner.

Who can stand on one foot the longest?

Clumps

Good ice breakers that are fun and non-threatening to shy people are hard to find. Many kids don't want to be singled out or have to move out of their comfort zone, and that is pretty much the definition of an ice breaker. Let me introduce you to Clumps. (Sometimes people call it Bunches.)

You will yell out a topic while people mill around and find the group in which they fit. This is the perfect example of a game you can explain the fun out of. Let your students talk and work out the details.

For example, if you want them in groups based on their favorite foods, don't say, "Chinese food over here in the corner and Mexican food on the left." Just say, "Get in groups based on your favorite foods. You know, Chinese, Mexican, and so on."

When everyone has found a group, go around and ask each group what they are. I'll give you quite a few examples of groups to call out. Don't use them all. Stop before the students want you to.

Say this

Everybody stand up and get ready to move around a little bit. I want you to get into groups based on what I say. Find your group quickly.

- *Get into groups based on whether you are right or left handed. Go!*
- *Get into groups based on your favorite food. It may be Chinese, Mexican, steak, etc.. (After the groups split up, say "What is your group? to each of them.)*
- *Get into groups based on school grade.*
- *Get into groups based on hair color.*
- *Get into groups based on shirt design.*
- *Get into groups based on your favorite hobby.*
- *Get into groups based on birth months.*
- *Get into groups based on your favorite sport.*
- *Get into groups based on your favorite pets.*
- *Get into groups based on shoe type.*
- *Get into groups based on how sleepy you are.*

Find a reason to text a student and write:
"I'm glad I'm your student pastor
(or teacher, parent, or friend)."

5

Questions Only

I love games that can be played at a moment's notice with no preparation at all. This is one of those games.

You can just pick two players at a time, or you can get three or four people on each team. Have two people face off at the front of room. The teams can line up behind each of the leaders.

The two people who are squaring off have to ask questions to one another. They cannot repeat a question. They can't pause for more than a second or two. They must simply ask questions back and forth to one another.

It may be fun to let the winner of each round continue until he or she is defeated. Remember, one of the keys to leading games well is to stop while it's still fun. Three or four rounds of this is probably enough.

Say this

I need three juniors on my left and three seniors on my right. The first two of you come right here and meet in the middle like you're in a Thunderdome death match or something. Please try to look fierce. You two put the "timid" in "intimidating."

You first two are going to have a conversation of just questions. That's it. Just ask one another questions back and forth. You can't repeat a question or pause for more than just a second. Also, they have to be more than one word questions.

Do you understand? Are you sure? See what I did there? Did I just do it again? Am I on fire or what?

Whichever team wins the best two out of three is Grand Major Champ.

If your salvation ever becomes anything less than mind-blowingly awesome to you, you need to think about exactly what salvation is again. Your Maker was also your ransom. Amazing!

Mental Ping Pong

Get two teams of three and have them line up at each side of your podium facing inward. We will have three rounds in this head-to-head battle.

With the first two contestants from each team faced off at the podium, explain that you will give them a category and they must take turns naming something that fits the category. The first person who either can't think of something, repeats an answer, or takes longer than three seconds to answer, loses.

For instance, if the category were ice cream favors, the first person might say "chocolate" and the other guy would say "strawberry" and then the "chocolate" guy would say "rocky road" and on and on until one of them fails. On a related note, I could really go for a banana split.

It might be nice to designate one of your volunteers to be the official three second buzzer guy. A simple "AAAAAAAHH" buzzer noise with his mouth will suffice.

When one of them wins, the next two contestants step up and name pro baseball teams, or whatever. Give the team a prize that wins the best two out of three. If a team wins in just two rounds, make a big deal about the last contestant on the losing team saving his group from the dreaded skunk.

Categories may include:

- Restaurants
- Stores in the mall
- Candy bars
- People in the room
- Things in a locker

Say this

I need three juniors and three seniors up here quickly. Juniors on my
left and seniors on my right.

I will give you a category such as "birds." You first two in
line will go head-to-head to see who's the greatest. We will
let our junior start us off and he might say something like,
"cardinal." Then the senior would say, "dodo bird." Then the
junior would say "chicken," and so on.

You lose by repeating an answer or taking longer than three
seconds to answer. We are going to play three rounds. Best
two out of three wins.

Okay, you first two are up. Your category is "things on a
playground." Junior, GO!

Cheapest way to feed a group of people...hot dogs.
Feeling fancy? Spaghetti.

7

Say Anything

This may be the simplest, no preparation, last minute class starter game of all time.

Get two contestants to the front of the room. Tell them their job is to say anything. They can literally say any word that is a person, place, thing, or idea. One person will start and then the other person will say something. They will go back and forth until one of them pauses for three seconds or repeats an answer.

For some reason this is way harder than it sounds.

After these two play a round or two, you will have someone in your crowd who says, "They are terrible. This is easy." Challenge that person to a competition from his seat. Then beat him silly with Old Testament Bible names, '90's sitcom actors, and hair metal album titles. You don't have all that useless stuff stored in your brain for nothing!

Chris and Lisa, step up here with me. When I say "go" I want you two to take turns saying anything. Say any person, place, thing, or idea without repeating one or pausing for more than three seconds.

There are literally billions of possibilities and I can almost guarantee you this will not last more than a minute.

Ready, Lisa? Go!

Give everyone a sucker with gum in the middle.
First person to blow a bubble gets a free toothache.

8

Invisible Chalkboard
aka
"Oh No You Dih-uhnt !"

You can play this with everyone or you can do it as an up-front game.

Two people should stand facing one another. When you say "go" each person should use her index finger to write out the alphabet on an "invisible chalkboard" in front of them. When they are done, they should throw their hands up and give a celebratory whoop.

After one round, before you let two more people do it say, "This time pretend like these are two people arguing and you can't make out what they are saying." It's really fun. By the way, when writing the alphabet gets old, have them write the numbers 1-20.

Say this

Jamie and Terri, step up here to the front of the room.

Are you two up for the challenge? I want you two to stand face-to-face and pretend there is an invisible chalkboard between you. One of you will write on one side of this chalkboard, and the other one will write on the other side.

I want you to use your index finger to write on the board when I tell you to "go." When I say, "Go" I want you to start writing the alphabet on your invisible chalkboard in front of you. When you get done, put your hands up in the air and let out a whoop so we will know you are done.

Give us a little whoop preview.

No cheating. Make sure you draw every letter. Don't touch the person in front of you.

Ready? Get set. Go!

Nice job. Give me two more competitors. And this time I want all of you to pretend these two are having a heated argument, but you can't hear what they're saying. Do your best to imagine them saying, "Oh no you didn't!"

Check out your local thrift stores for great deals on Nerf® blasters. It's not uncommon to pay 0.99¢ for a $20 gun! I should know since I own around four hundred Nerf guns. It's a start.

9

More or Less

I'll give you some weird trivia that involves numbers. Read the question and wait for responses. The kids will kind of murmur with the person next to them, which is awesome! This shows interest.

Choose a student to make a guess. Next, have another student guess whether or not the answer is more or less than the answer given by the first student. Give the winner a prize.

1. How many days would it take for you to count to a million by ones? (10 Days)

2. How many tennis balls are used during the two weeks at Wimbledon? (54,250)

3. How many airplanes are in the air at any given time over the US? (5,000)

4. How much does a medium sized dog cost its owner over the course of its life? ($6,565)

5. How many hairs are on the average red-haired person's head? (90,000)

6. How many teeth does a person have over the course of his life? (52)

7. When did the first iPhone come out? (June 29, 2007)

Say this

Does everyone see this Kit Kat bar? It may be yours. But do me a favor. If you win it, will you please break off one wafer at a time to eat it? Those people who just bite into the group of four attached wafers weird me out.

Kendal, you would eat this Kit Kat correctly, wouldn't you? How many days would it take for a person to count to a million by ones? (Give Kendal the chance to answer.)

Okay, Kendal, you say it would take _____ days to count to a million. Now choose someone in here to be your competitor. (He chooses Lauren.) Lauren, now I want you to say "more" or "less" depending on whether you think it would take more or less than _____ days to count to a million. What do you think? (Allow Lauren to answer.)

The answer is ten days. Great job _____! By the way it would take thirty-one years, 251 days, seven hours, forty-six minutes, and forty seconds to count to a billion. (You can google anything.) Eat this Kit Kat® responsibly! Who's next?

How guilty should you feel about folks who don't like pizza when you order pizza? About a loaf of bread and a pack of turkey-guilty. Perhaps a Lunchable® is in order. C'mon people, it's pizza!

Section 3

Team Building

Wacky Wedding

Divide groups into guys vs. girls. Give the girls five or six white trash bags, a roll of toilet paper, and a roll of white duct tape.

Give the guys five or six black trash bags, a roll of toilet paper, and a roll of black duct tape.

Each group needs to pick a bride or groom to dress. (NO clothes need to be removed!)

Give them fifteen minutes to design a wedding dress and tux respectively. Have some impartial judges pick the winner. (Let the redneck nuptials begin!)

Say this

Girls, you have fifteen minutes to take these items and make a wedding dress. Pick one lady to model it for us. Guys, you may use these things to dress up one of your friends in a tux. Get creative. Make sure everyone does some of the work. The wedding is in fifteen minutes. GO!

The weirder the prize, the more fun the game. Stock up on ramen noodles and cheap toys.

Iced Tee

Wet down two pairs of pants, two shirts, and maybe two pairs of socks at least four hours before your meeting. Put them in the freezer with wax paper between each item so they don't stick to one another.

Six hours later, they will be frozen solid. In four hours, they will be mostly frozen. If you can put them in the freezer the night before it is even better. It might be good to practice this with the clothes and freezer you will use. It's not an exact science. If you really get the clothes wet and freeze them for a long time it will take forever to thaw them.

Divide your group into two teams. Throw each team a shirt and a pair of pants. (It sounds cool when the frozen items hit the ground.) The first team that can get their clothes on someone in the group is the winner. They'll have to heat the clothes up with their hands to get them open.

Say this

Look at your hands. It's hard to believe those lovely mitts of yours are almost 100 degrees. It's time to put them to use.

(Throw the clothes in the floor on each side of the room.)

This is left side verses right side of the room. The first side that gets the clothes on one of your team members is the winner. The winning side gets Fla-Vor-Ice.® GO!

Live to defy the stereotypical lazy, immature, dangerous, goofy, shallow student pastor.

12

Cupper Upper

Hand each of the two contestants a stack of plastic or foam cups. There should be about five more cups than there are people on each team. Let the students choose who will be the "right side up" team. The other team will be the "upside down cup" team.

Next, have the students spread their cups around the room on the floor. "Right side up" team will obviously place their cups right side up and "upside down" team will turn their cups upside down. They can place them anywhere in the room.

When you say "Go," the students should hurry to their opponent's cups and turn them over so they are facing their team's way. Of course, the other team will go back and flip them the way he or she wants them.

Give your students thirty seconds to flip as many as they can. At the end of the time period count how many cups are right side up and how many are upside down. Whoever has the most is the winner.

Play again, letting the upside down team become the right side up team. It's only fair since I feel like it's easier to turn the cup on its head, don't you think?

Let's split down the middle of the room to make two teams. One group will be the "right side up cup" team and the other will be the "upside down cup" team. Give each person on your team a cup. There are a few extra. We will use them, too.

Which group wants to be the "right side up cup" team?

Next, I want you to spread your cups around the room on the floor. "Right side up" team will obviously place their cups right side up and "upside down" team will turn their cups upside down. Place them anywhere in the room.

When I say "Go," hurry to your opponent's cups and turn them over so they are facing their team's way. The other team will go back and flip them the way they want them.

You will have thirty seconds to flip as many as you can. At the end of the time period, we will count how many cups are right side up and how many are upside down. Whoever has the most is the winner.

Don't touch them after I say "stop" or we will clip your fingernails down to that terrible part.

Ready? Set? Go!

Try to fathom the vastness of God. Now take a moment to snicker at yourself and feel ashamed at the terrible job you did. BIGGER!!

13

Minefield

Tape off a large rectangle on the floor around 8 x 16 feet. Place approximately forty or fifty foam or paper cups in the rectangle. Blindfold your two contestants with a pair of swimming goggles you blacked out with duct tape. They make wonderful blindfolds that don't fall off or allow peeking.

Assign each competitor a person to talk them through the course. Everyone else is trying to throw them off by giving bad directions and causing distractions. If the contestant touches a cup…BOOM! That was them pretend exploding. Help them go back to begin again.

The first one to make it through the course without blowing up a landmine is the winner.

This is the best illustration in the world of the teen experience.

I have this area taped off. I need ten of you to grab five of these cups each and spread them out in the area I have taped off.

While they do that, I want Carrie and Ellie to put these blindfolds on. You will start at one end and make it to the other without touching a cup. Carrie, your partner is Barrett. Ellie, your partner is Caia. They will give you good directions. The problem is everyone else will try to mess you up by yelling bad directions.

If you touch a cup you "explode" and have to start again. Carrie and Ellie, get in your places. All you guys, do a good job of trying to mess them up.

Duct tape often leaves residue on carpet. Yes, I know this about duct tape because there is a permanent "three-point line" in front of the altar at my church that I will never hear the end of. On the other hand, painters tape sticks well and does not pull up carpet threads or leave gummy residue, most of the time!

14

﹚Six on a Brick﹙

If you are looking for a quick, fun, team-building game you're in luck. You will need a few bricks for this. You could also use flat landscaping stones or some other type of low, flat, strong surface that a person can stand on.

Break into groups of the same gender. If you have ten students in each group, lay ten bricks on the floor. Each group has to get all of its members off the ground and standing on the bricks for three seconds. Let each group have a turn.

If a group can't get everyone off the ground for three seconds, they are out.

Remove a brick every round. The players will have to start standing on one another's feet and holding on to one another to succeed. As long as they are being safe, let them get creative as the bricks disappear. If they can get ten people on a single brick, they should go down in history books.

Give each member of the winning team a ten-dollar bill. Who am I kidding? Give each winner a Lego® brick to represent their epic victory.

Say this

Everyone, do me a favor. Separate into guys and girls, and get into groups of ten. Some of you may have to be in more than one group to get the teams up to ten people.

Give me the first group of ten girls. See these bricks I have on the floor? Your job is to get your whole team off the ground for three seconds by standing on the bricks. You can stand on one another's feet, hold onto one another, or whatever you have to do to make it happen. Are you ready? See if you can do it, girls. Once everyone gets off the ground we will count to three for you.

Our first team of guys will go next. We will take a brick away every round.

Some things in your life will have to be left undone.
Do NOT let one of them be your family.

15

Antigravity Stick

You need a long, lightweight stick like a tent pole. You could also use a 10-foot piece of 1/2 inch PVC pipe if you are not into camping.

Have your kids stand shoulder to shoulder with elbows relaxed but their hands pointing like they're holding out two guns with their index fingers as the barrels. It should kind of look like they're signaling a touchdown in Australian Rules Football. (It's worth an Internet search. I love those guys.)

Students can get on both sides of the stick if they'd like. You should be able to get about eight people on a 10-foot stick if they get close.

Tell them you are about to lay a stick across their fingers. Their goal is to lower the stick to the floor with it resting on their fingers. BOTH INDEX FINGERS HAVE TO MAINTAIN CONTACT WITH THE POLE THE WHOLE TIME.

The stick will "mysteriously" rise. The lightest touch by a few people will send the stick frustratingly skyward. Soon, everyone will get it in gear and they will reach the floor.

Hey guys, give me about ten people standing shoulder to shoulder up here. Everybody keep your elbows at your sides and point your pointer fingers straight out. I will lay this PVC pipe across your fingers. If there is not enough room for everyone to get your fingers on it, I want you to come around and face these folks and put your fingers under the stick.

Everybody MUST keep their fingers in contact with the PVC pipe.

(They should realize by now that the PVC is moving upward.)

Is the PVC starting to float? Your job is to get it all the way to the ground. Remember to maintain contact with it at all times.

(Debrief when you get done.)

Ask things like:

- *Whose fault was it that the stick went up?*
- *What was the most frustrating thing you dealt with during this exercise?*
- *Why is it so hard to depend on other people?*
- *If you had to do this again, what would you change?*
- *What can you do to become a better teammate?*

If you've never grilled a peanut butter sandwich, you've kind of wasted your life, and you're basically calling Elvis a dummy with every passing day.

Section 4

Games in a Circle

16

Protect the President

This is a fast-paced dodgeball game. Success lies in having the right ball. You need a lightweight ball that is easy to throw and catch, and will not hurt at close range. Normal dodgeballs are a little too heavy and hard for this game. A good question to ask yourself is: *Would I bounce this off my mom's forehead at close range?*

Have everyone stand in a circle. (Notice I didn't say students. Your leaders should play, too.) Ask two people to stand in the middle of the circle. Pick one of them to be the president. The other person is the secret service agent.

It's the secret service agent's job to protect the president. The people in the circle should try to hit the president with ball. The agent should try to protect the president by staying between him and the ball, and by knocking the ball away.

If the president gets hit, the agent becomes president and the person who hit the president becomes the agent. Only explain this once. The players will get the hang of it quickly when they see it.

Okay, everybody circle up. Good job!

Congratulations, Ron! You have just been elected president. Come stand behind me. I'm the secret service agent.

(Toss the ball to Michelle.) Whoever hits the president takes my secret service spot and I become the POTUS. Good luck because I am fast as lightening and twice as wide!

Fire away!

If you need a quick "dodgeball," use a clean sock. Start at the opening, and roll the sock down tightly as far as you can. It makes a cool donut-shaped sock ball.

17

'Sit Quickly'

Count your people including yourself. Have that exact number of chairs placed in a circle, touching one another. The chairs must be armless and it's best if they don't slide. Have everybody sit down except for you—since you will be standing in the middle. You will try to sit down during the game. The people sitting want to keep that from happening. They do this by quickly sliding over into the empty chair. This will leave their chair empty. So, the person next to them will need to quickly slide over and so on.

The person in the middle will end up squashing a person or two till he gets in a chair.

You may have to help get the direction started, but when the students get the hang of it they can change directions and trick each other. If the middle guy gets a seat, the person he kept from sitting goes in the middle. The cool part of this is that it looks like a wave as it moves around the circle. The students will catch on quickly and it will get much faster and really tough for the middle guy to sit down.

If you have a guy who looks like he's enjoying "failing" and landing in the laps of the ladies a little too much, get a new middle man.

Hey everyone, let's get our chairs in a circle. I'll get a chair, too.

This is more of a "U" with an apostrophe. Let's get in a circle. (You stand in the middle of the circle when you can, leaving an empty chair.)

Okay, once we start the game I will try to sit down in a chair. You don't want to let me sit. So as I come over to sit, slide into the empty chair. As the person next to you slides, you need to slide quickly, too. You can change direction if you'd like at some point.

If I make it into a spot, whoever has the least fanny in a seat comes to the middle.

Okay, here I come.

Lock-ins are to youth ministry what earthquakes are to ancient pyramid builders. They creep on you and you simply try to survive them.

18

Body Part Musical Chairs

This is almost just like regular musical chairs, the famous sit-down-when-the-music-stops game. It's an entertaining time-filler that you can prepare for in just a few minutes.

Here's how to play:

Like regular musical chairs, put the chairs in a circle facing outward. Have one less chair than number of participants.

Before you start the music, call out a body part like "forehead."

Start the music and have everyone walk around the circle.

When the music stops, the last person with their forehead in a chair loses and is out.

Call out other things like—nose, elbow, back of your head, bottom of your right foot, etc...

Body part musical chairs will make regular musical chairs seem like a quilting bee by comparison. (Unless you're into quilting bees, which is cool.) It's actually so entertaining you don't have to put people out to keep it interesting.

Try these body parts, too: the tiniest tip of your pinky finger, all of your body, one hair on your head, an ear, elbows and knees, top of your head, top of thumbnail, etc...

Okay, everyone pick up your chair and let's arrange them in a circle facing outward.

This is musical chairs, but I will give you the name of a body part that you have to put in a chair when the music stops. If you can't find a chair, you are the loser and you have to compliment me. You know, say something really nice about me. It really shouldn't be that tough.

Here we go. Everyone stand up so I can remove a chair. The body part you have to put in the chair when the music stops is both your elbows. Pump up the jam, DJ! (That means start the music if you're a Free Will Baptist like I am.)

(Remember, I'm not a huge fan of games that disqualify people unless they go fast so people can get back in. You don't have to get people "out" for this to be fun unless it's a game that's meant to be watched, like an up-front game. We want PARTICIPANTS!)

No matter how awesome your activity is, the gospel is still the power.

19

Pass the Spoon

For this craziness, you need six or eight types of jarred baby food. Peas are a good choice, as is anything that starts with the words, "Turkey with...." You'll also need a few plastic spoons, one big spoon for passing, and some music you can pause.

Have everyone get in a circle and pass the big spoon around until you stop the music. Whoever has the spoon when the music stops, reaches in the bag of baby food without looking and takes a bite of the baby food they chose.

Don't be a drill sergeant when it comes to making someone eat something they don't want to. Have them ask for a volunteer to take their "medicine" for them. It's not like a spoonful of baby food will hurt them, but you don't want to make anyone too uncomfortable (or nauseous). Promise everyone a prize who plays to the end. Give participants a piece of gum when game is over.

Keep going until the one crazy guy says he likes it and eats the whole jar of really nasty stuff and ruins the intrigue.

Say this

Let's all get in a circle. No, this is a trapezium. Let's get in a circle.
That's better.

I will start some music and while it's playing we will pass this spoon around. When the music stops, the person with the spoon will reach into this bag and take a bite of whatever he or she chooses. It won't be bad. It's actual baby food. You survived it once. But don't worry, if you don't want to do it you may ask one of these fine gentlemen or ladies to take your place.

Here's the spoon. I'll start the music.

Never, ever make a person uncomfortable
unless they want to be singled out. This disqualifies
games like "Get Your Team Over the Fence." No
matter how nice your students are, it terrifies the
heavier people. I'm not just guessing about this.

20
Ezekiel 1:16 Game

Have everyone find a partner. Make your leaders play, too.

Once everyone has a partner, form two circles—one inside the other. You should be in the circle that your buddy is not in. Both circles have the same number of people in them, so the people in the outer circle will be a little more spaced out. (By "spaced out" I mean they will have room between them, not like "Whoa duuuuude.")

In a minute, you will play some music. When you start the music, have one circle walk clockwise and the other circle walk counter-clockwise. But before you start the music call out a command like, "foot to knee." That means when you stop the music, the two partners have to find one another and one of them has to put his foot on his partner's knee.

Start the music and let them walk a minute. At some point stop the music and enjoy watching the kids kick their buddies in the knee. I'm kidding! Remind them to be gentle.

Be creative in your commands: fist to fist, knee to backside, elbow to nose, head to head, calf to shoulder, pinky to pinky toe. Man, I have to play this Sunday!

You can play to get a winner by kicking the last couple out of the game each round, but it's more fun to let everyone stay in. You might make the slowest people eat a piece of sour candy for each loss.

Everybody find a partner. If you have trouble finding a partner raise your hand. We will hook you up. This is not a long-term relationship. Just identify a partner for the game.

Now, listen carefully. We will form two circles, one inside the other. You and your awesome partner should be in different circles. Let's get there now.

Okay, outside circle, when I start the music, you will walk counter-clockwise. Try it now. (Help them find their direction.) Good. Inside circle, you will walk clockwise. Try it now. Nice.

I will call out two body parts such as ear to elbow, and then start the music. When the music stops, you have to find your partner and put those two parts together. I promise it won't be embarrassing.

Here we go. Foot to knee. (Start the music) Start walking. Get ready. When it stops, don't be last.

Get a whiteboard as well as a marker in each hand. Start in the middle and write your name forward with your right hand and backwards with your left hand. Seriously, you can do it. Try it in the air right now. Aren't you awesome?!

Blindfolded Samurai

You will need a slightly confined space for this. If your area is vast (you lucky dog!), you can make it smaller by opening the legs on folding tables and placing them on their sides to cut down the room or even use them to make a hexagon Thunderdome of death. You can make a good hexagon area for about twenty people with six large folding tables turned on their sides with their feet facing outward.

You will also need a pool noodle cut in half (for swords). You'll need two pair of the non-nose covering swimming goggles. Use some duct tape to cover the glass on the goggles. These make great blindfolds.

Give one girl and one boy a sword and a blindfold. Have everyone get in the hexagon. The blindfolded samurai will try to whack everyone with their swords. When a person gets whacked, he leaves the circle. The last gender remaining in the hexagon with the samurai wins.

If the sword carriers have trouble finding victims when they get down to the last few folks, remove a table and slide the remaining tables back together to make the area smaller.

After a couple of rounds play a joke on the sword carriers. After everyone is out, keep yelling, "Swing higher, now lower. Harder!" Then have them remove their blindfolds to reveal that they have been made to look foolish. This will embarrass them and also make everyone uncomfortable as they wonder if they will be the next person tricked. *Bwahahaha*!

You know what, on second thought don't do this last part. Okay, do it, but use a couple of your secure volunteers.

Say this

I need a boy and girl who think they are amateur Jedi. Hey Beth and Rusty, take these blindfolds and swords. Put the blindfold on. Everyone stand up and get in this open area. These two visionless samurai Jedi will try to whack you with their swords. If you get hit, you are out. Leave the area.

We will make the area smaller as we go. Jedi, whack like crazy! These dudes are elusive. By the way, you are representing your entire gender. Who will be the last one alive? Ready? Go!

A volunteer who will not participate
makes an excellent doorstop. Of course,
so does an old broken flip flop. Show your
volunteers exactly what you want from them.

22
King of the Ring

You will need two halves of a pool noodle for this.

Have everyone stand in a circle. In the middle of the circle, one student will stand with one half pool noodle sword in his hand. The other half pool noodle will be in the floor in the center of the circle.

The player in the middle should walk around menacingly, daring someone to dash toward the middle to grab the other sword. If a person charges to grab the sword on the floor and the player in the middle whacks the person as she tries to grab the sword off the floor before she touches it, she must sulk back to the circle and sit out the rest of that round.

If the challenger touches the sword on the floor before the King of the Ring (person in the middle with the sword) whacks her, it is on! If the challenger touches the sword before she is hit, she picks up the sword in the middle of the room, the two swordsmen bow to one another, then they duel. The first one to hit his or her opponent anywhere besides the sword is the winner. He or she becomes the King of the Ring.

I have seen nights when no one has the guts to challenge the king so he has to kick the sword toward someone and back away a little to get an opponent. And I've also had matches where everyone charges toward the sword and it turned into a foam noodle bloodbath, so to speak.

You have to kind of play this by ear and adjust the rules to fit your situation. But no matter what, make sure there is some over-the-top, cheesy British movie bow and curtsy before the two swordsmen go at it.

Corey, catch this half noodle and step to the middle of the room with me.

Everyone gather around us in a circle. I will put this other half noodle on the ground. Corey, your job is to whack people when they try to get to the noodle. If someone touches this sword on the floor before they get whacked by you, then you two are going to duel. So, let me back up and let the fun begin. Who has the guts to go for the sword?

(Once someone has made it to the sword, continue with instructions.) Okay, you two face each another, take an honorable bow toward one another, then it's on. The first person to hit the other person somewhere on their body is the new reigning King of the Ring. Begin!

If you ever utter the words, "Hey, anybody want to play a game?" again, we cannot be friends. Students should be having fun before they realize they are playing.

23

Camera Spoon

This is a wonderful game you can easily play in a group of about fifteen or fewer. You can play it with more after you get the hang of it.

Hold up a spoon and say, "This is no ordinary spoon. This, my friends, is a camera spoon."

Explain that you'll leave the room and have someone go with you to make sure you don't peek. When you are out of the room a volunteer, it doesn't matter who, will take the spoon and hold it in front of someone, saying, "Click." Then you will come back into the room, look deeply into the spoon and tell the group whose picture was taken.

The trick to this game is that you'll have an accomplice in the room. The accomplice's job is to subtly mimic every move of the person who has had his or her picture taken. It may be helpful to have a signal that narrows the field immediately. Have them give you a smile if the picture is of a girl, and a frown if it's a boy—to help you narrow down your search. It might even be possible to have your accomplice point his foot in the direction of the person. But don't worry too much about the signals. If the accomplice mimics the person well, it won't be tough to pick them out.

If your accomplice gets his or her picture taken, have him play with his watch or do some other sign you work out ahead of time. Over-explain things to your accomplice and really work out the details. There's a little art to it, but it's so beautiful when you do it well.

It may help to have more than one accomplice. Not only will they help you find the right person, but if the kids catch on to one of your helpers you can have them leave the room and you'll still have an accomplice. If you happen to guess the wrong person, just say the camera was out of focus and clean the spoon, or blame it on bad photography.

One time, two friends and I went on a recruitment trip for a college and we played this game. Obviously, the kids were suspicious of my two friends (for good reason, they were my accomplices). So, I got brave and said, "I'll prove the camera is magic. I'll take them outside with me while you take the picture." When we got outside, my friends said, "What are you going to do now?" I replied, "I saw this 'mind reader' have his secrets revealed on one of those investigative shows one time. I think I can do it!" (Of course I also saw a show about how tightrope walking works one time and that did not go well for me OR the rope.)

I should have had another accomplice set up, but I decided to try to do like "good" mind readers and get the answer out of them slowly by their reactions to my dialogue.

First, I said, "Whoa, that's one ugly picture." Trying to tell who everyone looks toward and who looks offended, I said "Don't get me wrong. The person is not ugly. it's just not a good picture. They are kind of girly-looking." Laughter means it's a boy. Silence meant it was a girl. Then I noticed everyone seemed to keep looking in the direction of a couple of girls. I went with the quietest one trying not to attract attention. I guessed correctly. To their wild amazement they said, "How did you do that? Let me see that spoon." And I am "magic" forever.

This is the ultimate "STOP while you're winning" game.

Guys, this is a magic spoon. It's actually not magic, it's a camera. You can take this, hold it in front of someone, then say, "Click" and I can look at it and tell you whose picture was taken.

Seriously, who wants to try it? I'll leave the room; you take a picture of someone and I'll come back in and tell you who it was.

Does anyone want to come with me to make sure I don't peek?

(Leave so they can take the picture. Re-enter when they are ready for you.)

Let me see the spoon, I mean camera. Whew! That is gross! No, sorry. It was just some left-over chili on the spoon.

Oh, it's coming into focus. (Walk around holding the spoon next to people's faces as if you are comparing the image to their face. This will give you an opportunity to check out your accomplice and see who he is pointing out.)

Darrell, is it you? (If you miss it, blame it on being out of focus. Tell them to hold the spoon a little closer to the subject next time.)

Writing things on poster board with those really huge markers looks cool for some reason.

Section 5

Group Games Ending With a Winner

24

Pirates Attack

This is really fun to play at a casual gathering like a lock-in or retreat. You give the commands and the students follow them. And the commands are awesome.

I have seen different incarnations of this game. Make up your own commands if you can come up with them. There should be a Loch Ness Monster and mermaid in here somewhere.

In a location where you have plenty of room, have the students stand in an area facing you. When you say, "Captain on deck," everyone should snap to attention and salute. When you say "Port" everyone should shuffle to the left. When you say "Starboard" they should shuffle to the right.

When you say "Hit the Deck!" everyone should fall down on their belly. The last one down could be out if you want to get a winner, but it's fun to let everyone continue to play.

When you say "Six men rowing" the kids should get on their knees, one right behind the other, rowing with a pretend oar. If there are leftover people not able to get into a group of six, they are out. You can use any number of rowers, by the way.

Another group you can call is "Four guys eating." The students should sit in a circle with their legs crisscrossed, pretending to eat a bowl of beans. People who aren't able to form a group of four are out.

If you yell "Land Ho!" the kids should pair up with one of them on their knees in the front and the person standing behind them should put his hand to his forehead like he's gazing into the distance.

If you yell "Starfish" have five students lie on their backs with their feet touching one another, making a star out of their legs. Students who can't find a group of five are out.

Designate a couple of leaders to be pirates. When you say "Pirates Attack" they will run around and tag random people, getting them out.

Unfortunately, if I gave you exact words to say for this game, it would just be a big convoluted mess. I'm not worried though. You've got this!

You can poke the middles out of chocolate peanut butter cup candies if you are careful. And I'm not saying it makes you look cool but you can wear them on your eyes like glasses after that.

25 'Zombie Apocalypse

Before your time with your students begins, pull a couple of them aside. Tell them they have been infected with the zombie virus, but they shouldn't say anything about it. You might also want to explain how this is just for a game you will be playing and not a medical assessment.

If you'd like to be even sneakier, you can give two or three students a quarter before class with no other details. Then when you are ready to play say, "If I gave you a quarter, you are infected with the zombie virus. Sorry you had to find out this way."

A good rule of thumb is to have one zombie for every fifteen people, but you need at least two zombies.

When you say "Go," everyone should get up and move around, trying to avoid the zombies. As soon as you start, the zombies should be able to infect a person or two near them. Play until the whole room is infected. It might be fun to play the theme music from the Walking Dead during this game.

Before class began, I pulled two of you aside and said you had been infected with the zombie virus. When I say "Go," you two will be zombies. Zombies walk with completely stiff legs and with their arms out straight. They also moan. You can walk fast, but can't bend your knees.

If a zombie touches you, you'll become a zombie. You cannot leave this room. Who will be the last to be infected? When I say "Go," our zombies will begin their hunt. They may be sitting next to you now. By the way, there will be no impersonating a zombie. GO!

Last person alive wins...and then dies.

There's nothing cooler than being at the hospital to see a baby born. And later be around to help lead her to the Lord. And then years later—perform her wedding.

Stick around, Student Pastor!!

26

Cup Grab

This is a game that became famous when one of the Arsenal Football Club's players posted a video of the professional soccer team playing it. You can do an easy search for the video if I leave you confused.

You will need one plastic cone for every two people in your group. If you don't have cones left over from that soccer team you used to coach before you reclaimed your Saturdays to spend with your family, you can use plastic cups or something else a person can easily bend over and pick up.

Ask students to find a partner. They should face their partner and put a cone between them. They need enough room to bend over and follow your commands to grab the cone.

You will give them one word commands. The competitors will put their hands where you tell them. Mention parts like their knees, feet, ankles, thighs, head, shoulders and eventually say "CONE." When you say "CONE," each competitor should try to grab the cone before the other person gets it. Even when people put their hands on their head, they should probably stay bent over so they can be in position to grab the cone.

Whoever wins in each pair continues to the next round. Play until you get a winner.

Everybody find a partner and one of you two come get a foam cup (or plastic cone).

Good job. Now, put the cone/cup on the ground between you two. When I say "CONE!" the first one of you two who grabs it, wins.

I'll say some other things like "knees" or "head" and you have to touch your knees and heads when I say those things. But when I say "CONE," grab that thing like it's the Little Mermaid's voice box and you are Ursula the Sea Witch. (I probably shouldn't be able to use that reference so effortlessly.)

Here we go. Feet. Knees. Shoulders. CONE/CUP.

Okay. If you got the cone, you are still in. Find a new partner for round 2.

A large pizza will usually feed 3 adults as long as one of them is not me.

Odd or Even

Give everyone a penny. Have them pair up. The shortest person gets to call odd or even. Then they both flip their coins and catch them and see if they are even (both heads or both tails) or if they are odd (one head and one tail.)

The winner takes the loser's coins and finds a new partner. The losers sit down. Keep playing until you have the champion, who gets to keep all the money.

Say this

Do you pick up a penny if you see it on the ground? You don't, do you? Back in my day you could buy a soda and get into a movie for just five of those pennies, and now you walk past those little goldmines without a second thought. Well, not tonight.

Matt and Aaron, help me give away this cold cash. Everyone gets a penny.

Everybody get a partner. Whichever one of you is shorter gets to call odd or even. After the person makes the call, both of you flip your coins. If they are the same, they are even. If they are different, obviously, they are odd.

Short person, call odd or even. Then flip your coins. Loser give your penny to the winner and have a seat. Winner, find a new partner. By the end of this game, someone will be rich!

**On coins in circulation today,
Lincoln is the only president facing left.**

28

Fast Straw

Give everyone a straw. Have them put one end in their mouth. The object of this game is to see who can rotate the straw and get the opposite end in their mouth without using their hands. Video the contest and play it back in slow motion to blackmail the kids.

Have people jump up quickly when they get done. Let the two or three quickest compete in a quick straw duel.

Say this

Ask your volunteers to help pass out straws to everyone in order to get this part done quickly.

Okay everybody, put one end of your straw in your mouth. Now, using only your mouth, your job is to turn your straw around so the other end is in your mouth. DO NOT TOUCH IT WITH YOUR HANDS. If you drop it, you can start again (if you are down with the five second rule). Once you get it completely rotated, stand up.

Ready? Go!

(Pay attention to the top four.)

I need you four to come to the front of the room for the championship play-off. Everybody pick a favorite. Who do you think can pull this off? Ready? Go!

Check out recordsetter.com. You can set your own crazy record. I (my kids) actually set the record for chopping Pop Tarts in half TWICE, although it's been ripped from us again. You can watch our video there.

29

Peeps®
Spitting

Yes, it's exactly as it sounds. You need a cheap plastic drop cloth (if you're a sissy), some Peeps® marshmallow candies, and a tape measure (if you want to set a record to beat next time).

Establish a spitting line, pass out the Peeps®, and let the fun begin—one person at a time. Actually, there is one more thing. When people get ready to play, have them step up to the line with their Peep, name it, and angrily bite the head off it before they spit it for distance.

Change things up by placing a plastic drop cloth along with a bucket on the floor. Pass out the Peeps® and fire away at the bucket one at a time, this time shooting for accuracy. If you can record a round on your phone and play it back to the group in slow motion, you'll have some serious entertainment.

Okay guys, I hope you like Peeps®, but if you don't it's no big deal because these Peeps® aren't for eating. These were bought for spitting.

As you can see, I have a line on the floor with plastic laid out in front of it. Jason, come over here. Take this Peep®. Look at him in his little wax eyes. Name him for us. (Allow Jason to name his Peep®.)

Okay, angrily bite off "Eric's" head and see how far you can spit it. Don't you dare step over the line! Don't hold back. Eric can handle it.

The other day on ESPN, I think I heard them say the unofficial Peep® spitting record was fifteen feet! (Jason spits) Not bad! Who thinks they can beat that? There are five Twixes (informal pluralization of one of my favorite words) on the line for this challenge.

**Did you know Peeps® eyes are made out of wax?
I'm not sure if that's cool or disgusting.**

Gorilla–Man–Gun

This is Rock, Paper, Scissors using your whole body. Players pair up and stand back-to-back. On the count of three they turn (jump around quickly) and are either a gorilla, man, or gun.

If one chooses to be a gorilla, both hands are raised into the air in a fierce manner and an equally fierce growl is given.

If he or she chooses to be man, a hand is placed on the chin with a thoughtful furrowed brow, while saying, "Hmmm."

And if the choice is a gun, point a finger, while shouting, "Bang!"

This is how it goes: Gorilla beats man, because he's stronger. Man beats gun, because he can control it. And gun beats gorilla, because it can shoot him.

Draw a simple explanation on a whiteboard with one line that has a gorilla, the word "beats," then a stick man figure. On the next line draw a man, the word "beats," then draw a gun. On the last line draw a gun, the word "beats," then draw a gorilla.

The winners of this game go to the next round and the losers sit down. In case of a tie, both people stay in the game, but watch out for funny business like both of them becoming a gun every time just to move to the next round. To eliminate this possibility, have a rule that says if there are two ties in a row then they are both out. Continue playing until there's a champ.

By the way, if you are not a fan of guns you can play Gorilla, Man, Banana. The sign for banana is making a banana peeling motion.

Brian come up here and play rock, paper, scissors with me really quickly. One, two, three—"Bang!"

That's too easy. Let's make this a little more awesome. Get back-to-back with me. Let me show you Gorilla. Ready? One, two, three...ROAR. Try it with me. One, two, three... ROAR.

Okay, next is Man. You put your hand on your chin in a thoughtful manner and say, "Hmmm." Try it with me. One, two, three, "Hmmm."

The last one is Gun. Ready? One, two, three, BANG.

This is how it goes: Gorilla beats man, because most gorillas are stronger than most men although I think I could take most gorillas not named Harambe. Man beats gun, because he can control a gun. And gun beats gorilla, because a gun can shoot a gorilla.

Randy come get back-to-back with Brian and let's see who is the man! Ready? One, two, three, GO!

Great job. Now everyone get back-to-back. You tie, you die. Here we go. One, two, three, "GO!"

If you're still in, find a new partner.

Hold the air that is in your mouth under as much pressure as you can (don't pass out). You may even hold your lips shut with your fingers. Click your tongue on the roof of your mouth a few times. Open your mouth and watch carefully for smoke. Cool, huh?

Lady and the Tramp

I use the word "finesse" often with my students. Young people are not known for finesse. Finesse is a complete mystery to young men specifically. They are experts at kicking a ball as hard as they can, but a well-placed touch pass in front of an open goal is not as simple.

This peculiarity in students makes tedious games like Lady and the Tramp really fun to watch.

You will need a box of uncooked spaghetti noodles. If you have a very large group, you'll need a few boxes. Have your people pair up and give each group a noodle.

The two people should carefully hold the ends of the noodle, making a little noodle bridge between them. When you say "Go" the pairs should walk around trying to protect their noodle while chopping everyone else's in half.

If the noodle breaks, whether it is a self-induced break or a karate chop, the team is out. The last team standing wins.

If this gets boring, you might want to have the teams put each end of the noodle in their mouths. Play it the same way. This is where the name comes from.

Everyone find a partner. Are you standing beside them? Find out what their middle name is.

Now, one of you come get a spaghetti noodle.

Each of you grab your spaghetti noodle by the two ends. Be careful not to break it. Our motto is, "You break your noodle and we say 'toodles.'" Sorry, that's actually not our motto.

When I say "Chop Suey," go around and try to break other people's noodles while keeping yours intact.

If yours breaks, have a seat in shame.

Ready, Chop Suey. (Get a winner.)

Great, we have a winner. Here are your two sticks of Sprees®.

Hey guys, if you love your old student pastor will you help me pick up all these spaghetti fragments? Let's especially get the big ones. Our mice will get the little pieces.

Have you ever tried spinning a pillow on your finger? It's amazingly simple. Once you master a pillow go for a tray. I have no idea why you'd want to do this.

Evolution

In honor of the fact that if evolution were true we should be wading waist deep in fossils of missing links. But since there is not one single quality specimen in existence, let's play "Evolution."

This is basically a rock, paper, scissors tournament. We will use the evolutionary order of egg, chicken, monkey, caveman, and cannonball to find a winner. (By the way, one of my most beloved leaders has the nickname "Cannonball." I hope you have a "Cannonball." Make him or her the top of your evolutionary ladder.)

Everyone starts out as an egg. To start the game, everyone stands up and when you say "Go" the players should place their hands above their heads with the tips of their middle fingers touching. It should make an egg shape with their arms above their heads. Contestants walk around to find another "egg" while yelling, "I'm an egg!" When two "egg people" come together, they play rock, paper scissors to see who moves up the evolutionary chain. The winner becomes a chicken. The loser goes back to an egg. Survival of the fittest you know. If they tie, they play again.

The winner makes chicken wings out of his arms while yelling "I'm a chicken" and looks for another chicken to play while the loser goes back to being an egg. The chicken who beats another chicken becomes a monkey. The motions for monkey are the international monkey motions. Scratch the sides of your tummy with your knuckles.

The monkey who wins becomes a caveman. He hunches over in a knuckle-dragging manner and looks for another caveman to play. The loser goes all the way back to be an egg.

The first caveman who wins is <u>insert beloved volunteer's name here</u>. He or she is the top of the evolutionary chain. The first person who makes it to that position should yell out, "I am <u>insert your leader's name here</u>." Crown the winner with riches or a bag of Twizzlers®.

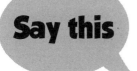

Jimmy come here quickly and play me in rock, paper, scissors. This is the way we do it. "Rock, paper, scissors, shoot." See if you can beat me.

We will have a rock, paper, scissors tournament but we'll start out as eggs. Put your hands up in an egg shape like this and say "I'm an egg" until you find another egg to play against. Whoever wins between the two of you becomes a chicken. (Show the chicken motion.) The loser always goes back to egg and finds another egg to play. If you are a chicken, find another chicken to play. If you're a chicken and you win that match you become a monkey. (Show the monkey motion.) If you lose you go back to be an egg.

Next in line is the caveman. You guys know how to be a caveman. (Do a caveman motion.) If you win that competition you are <u>insert beloved leader's name here</u>. That makes you the champ. Make sure you yell, "I am _____." We have a huge prize for the champ. That prize is pride in knowing you are the absolute top of the evolutionary ladder...which is actually a lie. There should be a fossil record so incredible it makes our heads spin and yet there is not one credible missing link. So, you are the king of lies. Well, you will also get some Twizzlers®.

Someone with art skills run up here and draw our evolutionary order on this board. It's egg, chicken, monkey, caveman, man. You only have fifteen seconds to draw them. It doesn't have to be museum quality. Let's Play!

Section 6

Up Front Games Ending With a Winner

33

Sock It to Me

This is a fun game because it involves a little risk. You'll need a bucket, net, or target and some pretty good prizes. It doesn't have to be a private jet or anything, but more than a stick of gum.

As students chooses to play, when it's their turn, they will remove their sock and skillfully throw it at the bucket or target you have provided.

If they hit the target they get the prize. If they miss, you keep their sock. They can go double or nothing with the other sock, but be a stickler and do not return missed socks.

It might be fun to have a plastic bag on hand to keep your trophies and display them somewhere in the room. If you think you have a parent who might not see the humor in you stealing her child's sock, return it to the killjoy (after you pull out a trophy thread).

Other options for returning the socks (so you won't get fired):

- Wet them down, freeze them, and return them at the next meeting.
- Return the sock if the student will put the sock in his or her shoe, but not on his or her foot.
- Return the sock if the student will wear the sock on the outside of his or her shoe.
- Return the sock if the student will wear the sock on his or her ear.
- Return the sock if the student will wear the sock as a glove for the rest of class.

Does anyone feel like taking a risk today? I have some huge prizes you can win, but it's risky. If you lose, it will cost you your socks. I'm serious! I'm coming after your stinking socks.

I have a bucket here that I will set where we can all see it. If you would like to win a prize—when it's your turn, take off your sock and toss it in the bucket. If you make it, you get an awesome prize. If you miss the bucket, I keep your sock.

Who's first? By the way, I'm not messing around, you will not get this sock back if you miss. And, you have to throw it from your chair.

Let's start over here at the right side of the room. Lauren, do you want to try? You can wad it, roll it, or whatever you'd like.

Have you ever ripped up a dollar bill in front of kids when teaching about greed? Trust me, it will be the best dollar you've ever spent. I ripped up a 5 dollar bill one time and we had to resuscitate a kid.

Mad Hops

We try to keep all the activities in this book simple. Minimal preparation and low cost are our focus. But there's a good chance you have a simple way to get pictures from your phone to a big screen. Dongles (I promise I didn't make that word up) that allow you to go directly from your phone to the projector or screen are common, incredibly handy, and not too expensive.

Choose two or more guys to go head-to-head in a jumping competition. When you say "Go," for about fifteen seconds, they should start doing everything they can to make sure their feet are off the ground while you snap about ten pictures. They need to jump as high and fast as they can. Emphasize the importance of jumping high and fast.

Snap the ten pictures with your phone which should take about fifteen seconds. If you have the ability, attach your phone to a projector and look at the pictures one at a time while counting the number of times each contestant is off the floor in your photos. The student who is in the air the most is the champ.

Make sure you zoom in on feet that are close to the floor. Also, zoom in on really weird-looking faces that the jumpers make.

Who are my two guys in here who think you can jump the highest? How about Barry and Terry. You two come up here to the front of the room. We will see who has the maddest hops. (At least that's the way we said people could jump high back in 1992.)

This is what I want you guys to do. When I say "Go," I want you to start jumping as high and as fast as you can. I want you to jump for about fifteen seconds. I'm going to take ten pictures of you two while you're jumping. Then we will go back through the pictures and you will get a point for every picture where your feet are off of the ground.

Just think to yourself, "I want my feet on the ground for as little time as possible." So, jump as high and as fast as possible.

Are you guys ready? Set. Go!

(Take the pictures.)

Okay, Amanda, you keep up with how many times Barry is off of the ground. Donna, you count for Terry. Let's go through these.

(As you swipe through the pictures it should be easy for you to zoom in on weird faces or feet that are close to the floor.)

If you chomp a wintergreen Life Saver® in a completely dark room it really does make a little green spark, AND makes your mouth minty fresh!

Yay/Boo

Pick a contestant and blindfold him. Place a bag of candy somewhere in the room on the floor. Have enough candy in the bag for everyone to get a piece. Fun size candy bars work nicely. Be sure to make a joke about how they are actually the least fun size.

Set a timer for thirty seconds. There are some pretty good countdown apps but there are even better-looking countdown videos on YouTube.

Spin your contestant around a couple of times and turn him loose. As he moves, have everyone either cheer or boo to tell him if he's going in the right direction. If he gets to the candy in time celebrate like maniacs and give everybody a piece of delicious goodness.

Say this

Oh my goodness, what do we have here? It's just the absolute best mix of fun size candy bars in the history of mankind. Why do they call these little ones "fun size"? They're actually the least fun size. But seriously, would you all like to put these wasted calories in your bodies? Diane, it's up to you. Do you guys have faith in her?

Put this fashionable blindfold on. You look like a million bucks. I'm going to put this bag somewhere in the room. I have thirty seconds on the clock. I'll let you spin around a few times, and when I say "Go" everyone will cheer when you're headed toward the candy. Let's practice. Cheer like she's going toward the candy. (Let them cheer.) When you're headed away from the candy they will "boo." Everyone boo.

(Quickly run the bag around the room making a little noise and place the candy in a hard-to-find place.) Okay, spin around three times and we'll start the clock. GO!

(Go crazy if she finds it. If she doesn't, make the kids give her a half-hearted cheer for trying and either pass out the candy anyway or try again at the end of your meeting.)

My favorite blindfold is a pair of cheap swimming goggles with duct tape covering the inside of them. They are stylish and utilitarian.

Water War

You'll need a deck of cards and about eight paper cups with a big thimble full (or two) of water in each of them and two cups half full (or half empty) of water.

Pick your two contestants and set four small cups and one large in front of each of them. Give each player half of the deck of cards. The players will flip the cards over one at a time. Whoever has the highest card throws one of his small cups in the face of the loser. If they both flip the same card, they can either both throw water or they can each flip another card. It's up to you. The first person to win five rounds is the champ.

The real winner is the crowd who gets to watch these two soak one another. Hey, it's just water. It dries and doesn't stain (most of the time).

(Have your four small cups with a small amount of water in each, and your one cup that is half-full set up and ready for each player you will call. Also, have a deck of cards to split to give each person half the deck.)

Say this

Who is not afraid of a little water? I need two people for this game. You two guys are perfect. Come sit at each side of this table.

You will play "War" with these cards. You can shuffle up your half of the deck if you'd like. When I tell you to flip a card, I want you to take your top card and flip it over at the same time. Whoever has the higher card gets to throw a cup of their water in the other person's face. We will play until someone has thrown all of their water. Save the big one for last.

Here we go.

Present the gospel at every service—TWICE!

37

Bucket Ball

Bucket Ball is the Michael Jordan of games. Did you ever see Bozo play the grand prize game? Yes, I know he was a little creepy and I'm scared of clowns too, but he had a pretty cool game.

You need five shallow buckets or plastic bowls. You can space these buckets out on the floor or even screw them to a 2 x 4 for a more permanent playing surface. Put them about two feet apart in a straight line. If your buckets are big or deep you may want to spread them further apart.

The player gets to stand right up against the first bucket. They will be able to basically bend over and lay the ping pong ball in the first two buckets. It gets tougher quickly.

These are the rules. You have to answer a question to earn each ball you will throw. If you make it in a bucket, you can take the prize and be done. If you go for the next bucket and miss, you lose everything. This is not gambling. It's… consequences. Actually, I think it would become gambling if you charged them to play. (I'm pretty sure that means I'm a Vegas high roller every time I see one of those stuffed animal claw machines.) This little risk is what makes this game exciting.

Choose a kid to stand with his feet touching the first bucket. He has to answer a question to earn his first ping pong ball. I use the plan of salvation. Like this:

Bucket One: True or false: Everyone in this room has done wrong. (True)

Bucket Two: Because everyone has done wrong, do we deserve a pizza *(or other awesome treat of your choice)* or punishment? (Punishment)

Bucket Three: There was one person who never did anything wrong. What's His name? (Jesus)

Bucket Four: Even though Jesus never did wrong, what did people do to Him? (They crucified Him.)

Bucket Five: If we make Jesus the Lord of our lives and repent, will He make us clean? (Yes)

This is the same basic gospel I walk people through when they want to give their lives to Christ.

As the students make baskets, the prizes get bigger. For example: bucket one=handshake, bucket two=piece of gum (.50 cent prize), bucket three=candy bar ($1.00 prize), bucket four=box of Twinkies ($3.00 prize), bucket five=$15 Starbucks card ($15.00 prize.) I know that sounds a little expensive, but you won't have to give away many of the big prizes. If they can make it into bucket five easily, your buckets are too big or too close together.

You'll see. People miss. People stop. You won't have to give away lots of big prizes.

You can also play this with inflatable pool floaty rings and a beach ball. Tie the rings together with strings and play the same way.

Be a stickler. If they miss, they are done. All they get is a smattering of applause on the way back to their seats.

Say this

Who wants to win fame and fortune here?

Nick, come put your toes right against this bucket for me.

This is how it works. You earn ping pong balls to throw by answering questions. You can stop anytime and take your prizes. But if you miss, you lose everything. There are no second chances.

Here we go. True or false: Everyone in here has done wrong. (True)

Good Job! Here's your ball. Try for bucket one. (If they miss it, give them a smattering of applause.)

(If they make it), Great job. Would you like a handshake from Larissa or would you like to go for bucket two? Don't forget, if you miss, you lose.

Okay, bucket two: Because we've all done wrong, do we deserve punishment or pizza? (Punishment)

(If they make it), It's getting tougher. Do you want this pack of Hubba Bubba Gum or do you want to go on?

Bucket three: There was one person who never did wrong. What was His name? (Jesus)

(If they make it), Nice. Would you like these share-size Reese's Cups® and go home, or do you want to go for the impossible dream that is bucket four?

It's getting crazy in here. Bucket four: Even though Jesus never did wrong, what did people do to Him? (Crucified Him,) Good luck, you will need it like you never have before.

(If they make it), OH. MY. GOODNESS. This is unprecedented. Do you want to take this whole, still warm, pizza or do you want to go for bucket five and the Beats Headphones (they were donated)? Remember, I'm not the Lord. There are no second chances with me.

(If they go for it), Okay, if we make Jesus the Lord of our lives and repent, will Jesus make us clean? (Yes)

Here it is, people. Can it be done? (If they make it, go crazy.)

**Do your best to only do things
that are going to last for eternity.**

38

Who's The (Wo)Man?

Have two to four volunteers leave the room with some kind of strong candy. It could be hot or sour or both. Let one of them fill his mouth with the Fireballs®, Hot Tamales, Sour Patch Kids® or Cry Babies®. When they come back in, go down the line one at a time and let the students who are watching applaud for the student they think has the candy in his mouth.

Make sure to tell the competitors all to keep their mouths closed and to look guilty. They are trying to fool the class. After a few painful moments, have the guilty party step forward.

Say this

You four students, take this sour candy and step out of the room. Pick one person among you to put it all in their mouth. Then quickly come back in and stand at the front of the room. I want all of you to look guilty.

When you come back in, we will go down the line and vote on whom we think is the guilty party. Don't lollygag out there. Go do it, you awesome guinea pigs!

Do you have any idea what a wonderful idea the apple peel was? It tastes okay. It keeps the apple fresh forever. It even looks beautiful. I'd have never thought of that! God is so neat.

Greed

This could also be called "All the Prizes You Can Carry."

Choose a person to come to the front. Have a bunch of prizes (candy bars, candy, toys, gift cards, bicycle parts, etc..) very handy. Get just a few feet away from the player. You should be close enough to toss the prizes gently to the contestant.

Explain that the student can win prizes all day long if he chooses to and has the skill.

You will toss prizes at the contestant until he says "stop" or lets something hit the ground. He can stop any time he wants and keep all he catches. However, if anything hits the floor he loses everything!

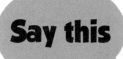
Say this

Donnie, come up here and stand with me. Do you like stuff?

I'm about to give you an opportunity to win some of it. I will throw stuff to you, and you get to keep all that you can catch. But if you drop anything, you lose everything. That means you need to tell me to stop when you have enough.

Prizes get a little better as we go. Here it comes. Yell, "Stop!" when you're done.

See who can do the best job of laughing
without smiling. It's incredibly funny.

40

Quick Clothespin

Stores usually sell clothespins in bunches of fifty. If your budget allows, buy two sets of them.

Get a couple of contestants, put thirty seconds on a timer, and see how many clothespins each of them can attach to themselves before time runs out. They can put them on the edge of their shirt, or in their hair, or wherever!

Our record is thirty-six. Good luck!

If this gets boring, tell them they have to attach them to their heads to get credit. That includes their mouths, ears, hair, etc.

Perry and Darius, come to the front of the room.

I have thirty seconds on the timer. How many of these clothespins do you think you can get attached to yourselves in that time?

I think it's impossible to get them all on you. There's a major prize if you can get them all attached to you in some way. Go!

Email me questions, ideas, or gift card vouchers at jondforrest@gmail.com.

41

Bottle Flip

Cool things come and go in phases. I hope by the time you are reading this, the bottle flip has become blasé. Unfortunately, I have a feeling we will be hearing the incessant thwack of bottles hitting the table for centuries to come.

If you are not familiar with the Olympic sport of bottle flipping, let me explain it to you. You leave about 1/4 to 1/3 of a water bottle full when you are drinking it and put the lid back on. Then you toss the bottle, have it rotate once, hoping for it to land on its bottom.

If you missed the original bottle flip video, it is worth a search. Be careful when you search "talent show water bottle flip" since there have been many imitators. The original and best one, has awesome music, and no cussing. If you have a way to show videos, play the original for your group. Then choose a player to reenact the video. Play it again in the background while your student walks around like the guy in the video. When the music stops, your contestant should flip the bottle, land it perfectly, and become immortal just like the talent show kid.

There are two types of people in the world. There are people who will lead this game and have multiple people toss the bottle until they get a winner. Most people are this kind of leader.

And then there are people who will only have one contestant try the bottle flip. This type of leader will buy an incredible prize, make a huge deal about the one contestant who gets to try the bottle flip, and if the player misses, he will throw the $6 cupcake he had for a prize in the trash. I like this leader. It ups the ante.

We have a coffee place in my area that makes cinnamon rolls the size of your head (I love you so much, Golly G's). I bought one last week and gave a kid the chance to win it. He missed. I threw the cinnamon roll away and thought my kids were going to tie me to a pole by my hands and feet and feed me to King Kong. A kid actually dug it out of the trash and ate it! When I saw that, I knew I was doing something right. I had their attention.

Which kind of leader are you?

A couple of weeks after you play this for the first time, you should get one of those big water cooler dispenser jugs. Put a little water in the bottom of it, tape the lid on well, and then MEGA-size this game. Double the prize! Be aware that if the student loses and you throw away that kind of prize you may have a "Lord of the Flies" style riot on your hands. Good luck!

Say this

Check out this video. (Show the talent show bottle flip video.)

Who thinks they can recreate this video tonight? Barney, come up here and give it a shot. I'm going to play the video again. You will walk around just like the guy in the video and when the music gets to a crescendo and stops I want you to flip this bottle onto that table, win this cake, and become immortal. Actually, you'll still be mortal, but it will be really cool.

Oh, and by the way, if you don't land it, this cake is going in the trash. This is a one-time deal. Barney, we call that tingling in your gut "pressure." Here we go!

Look up Post-It® mosaics.

42

Egghead

Go out to your barn and gather a dozen fresh eggs. For the few of you city slickers who don't have access to fresh eggs, I guess you can go to the store and buy a dozen eggs (but they're not the same). Hard boil seven of the eggs. Let them cool. Place them back in the carton.

Pick two contestants and give them a trash bag to cover their clothes. Rip head and arm holes for them. Put a plastic drop cloth on the floor. This won't get very messy, but might get a little eggy.

Explain to the students that you have hard boiled most of the eggs in the carton but a few of them are still raw. They will choose the eggs, one at a time and bust them on their forehead. The first person to get three raw eggs loses.

Make sure they bust the egg sideways on their forehead. If they hit it on the end of the egg, it might give them a concussion. Tell them not to mess around. They should really smack it on their head.

Also, the eggs can change colors a little when they are hard boiled so don't let the student look at them for a long time. They need to choose a random egg pretty quickly. Have a few antibacterial wipes handy for clean-up.

Can I have two brave volunteers? Guess not. Will and Michael, you two are perfect. Come here and put your head and arms through these trash bags.

I have hard boiled most of the eggs in this carton. You two will pick an egg, one at a time and smack it on your forehead. Don't knock yourself out, but don't mess around with it either.

The first person to find three raw eggs loses. Who do y'all think is going to win? I would say, "All of us watching."

Are you memorizing Scripture?

43

Split or Steal

There is a weird game on British television called "Golden Balls." It's worth a google search. At the end of the game there is a pot of money that two contestants can either split or steal. They talk it over and then, hidden to the other player, they choose a ball that says either "split" or "steal." They are basically playing crazy mind games with one another.

If they both choose "split," they split the money down the middle and each go home with half. If one chooses "split" and the other chooses "steal" the contestant who chooses "steal" gets all the money. If they both choose "steal," no one gets the money and they walk away empty-handed.

All kinds of crazy psychological games and lies go on as they try to convince the other player to split the money.

If your budget allows, buy a pizza and play this between two of your students. It might be helpful to watch a clip from the show so they can get the gist of the game. A quick search on YouTube will bring you a clip of this game. Use a bag of candy if you can't get your hands on a pizza.

Say this

Hey Ellie and Carrie, come sit in these two chairs I have facing one another at the front of the room.

Check this out. (Place a delicious pizza in a box between them on a table.) This pizza may be yours. You might decide to split it. Or you might decide to take the whole thing. We will find out.

This is what I want you to do. I have two cards here for each of you. One says "split" and the other says "steal." In a minute, after you talk it over, you two will choose a card (keeping it secret from the other person). If you both choose "split" you will split the pizza and walk away with half. If one of you chooses "split" and the other one chooses "steal," the one who chooses to steal gets the whole thing. If you both choose "steal," neither one of you gets the pizza and we will eat it in front of you in a torturous way.

Of course, I would never condone lying, but this is a game and I'm not sure how I feel about some mind games and deception in this one instance. I wonder how you all feel about it. I guess we will see. So, you two talk about what you will do for a minute and then we will have you choose a card and reveal it to us.

(You may have to help the conversation along. And if they seem to just be going with honest straightforward answers throw a little doubt in there by saying, "You know she'd say those exact words if she were going to steal this from you.")

Okay, choose an answer, but don't show it yet. I want you to reveal them at the same time. Do you have it ready? Okay, ready, set, show us.

(Follow up by asking the class what they would've done. How do they feel about lying for a game like this? Would it be okay to lie on a show like "Survivor?")

Section 7

Big Starters
(aka Leftover Stuff)

44

Drop Cloth

You will need a tarp or large sheet that people can't see through for this. Quickly go around the room and let everyone say their name. Once is enough if they say it clearly and loudly.

Next, split the room in half. These are the two teams. Have a couple of your leaders hold the tarp up between the two teams so they cannot see one another at all. You may have to arrange your students differently if your sheet isn't big enough to hide the students on each side. They won't mind sitting legs crossed on the floor for a few minutes.

When the tarp is in place, let each team pick a contestant to walk up to the middle of the tarp and stand ready. When both sides are ready, count "3, 2, 1, DROP!" When you say "DROP," your leaders should drop the tarp between the two contestants who haven't been able to see one another. The first student to correctly say the other student's name is the winner.

They get a point for their team. It might be cool to have a big bag of candy for the winning side.

You might want to change up this game by playing with two people on each side. It might be easiest to have one person do the yelling on each team, but it might work to have a free for all. Maybe you could suggest people just start yelling out names of the other team before the curtain falls. Or maybe you could say, "Before we drop the curtain this time see if you two can give each other a high five without seeing one another. I'll count you down. 3, 2, 1." We're brainstorming here people!

(Have two of your trusted workers on standby with the big tarp or sheet and a chair for each of them to stand in.)

Okay, everyone listen closely to me. We will start here at Miranda. As we go around the room, say the name you want to be called. Say it loudly and don't mess around. I want us to get this done in just a few seconds. Let's get a rhythm going. Just go boom, boom, boom. Go Miranda.

(Once everyone has said his or her name, continue with instructions.) I'm splitting the room in half right here (pick a spot close to the middle of your room. It doesn't have to be exact.) Get on your side of the room. I have Matt and Aaron here with a tarp. They are setting up their chairs so they can hold the tarp and you can't see the other side of the room. Each side pick a person to come stand close to the tarp in the middle. I'll say "3, 2, 1, drop." When I say "drop," they will drop the tarp and the first of the two people at the tarp to say the other person's name gets a point.

We will play 5 rounds. Whichever side has the most points at the end of the game gets this bag of M&M's®.

Do not judge the success of your youth ministry based on the number of bowling trips you take. Ministry is one student, one moment at a time.

45

Cookie Unicorn

This is one of those cool games that you can bring back from time to time and see if you can beat your old record.

You can play this with two teams of two. Have one person lie down so the other can stack cookies, crackers, or whatever is handy on the other person's forehead.

Make sure everyone can see what's going on. If you don't have many rows of chairs the students may lie on the floor.

A fun variation is to let the person stack the cookies on the person's entire face. It **is** legal for the onlookers to try to make the human table laugh. You can't spell "face full of Oreos" without f-u-n.

I need two people up here with me. Athletic ability is not required and I prefer that they not be wearing dresses or kilts.

Okay, I need one of you to lie down on your back. Make your forehead as flat as possible. I have a pack of Oreos—Double Stuff of course. To the non-lying down contestant say, "You will stack Oreos on her forehead until they fall over. Take your time. We will count how many remain stacked. In the words of UFC referee John McCarthy, "Let's get it on."

Crowd, feel free to try to get this human table to laugh by saying funny things. You might be next and the winner gets all the Oreos we've put on people's heads. Oh, okay. You get a new, unused pack of Oreos! When the Oreos fall say, "Oh man, not bad! Who can beat that? Winner gets their very own bag of Oreos to eat."

**Each side of an Oreo has twelve flowers on it.
Each flower has four pedals.
And each little flower is delicious.**

46

Tissue Issue

Grab a couple of those high quality single-ply rolls of church toilet paper from the bathroom. Pick a student to leave the room. While the student is outside, pick a person to hide the toilet paper. Here's the catch. The person has to unroll the entire roll off the spool and hide it on their person the best they can. They only have one minute to do this! There should be some fierce unrolling.

Have the student leave the cardboard tube in the middle of the floor. Bring the contestant back in the room and let them walk around and hand the tube to the person they think is hiding the toilet paper. Have some grace when it comes to the clock on this one. Let the hider have a fighting chance.

Casually move to the center of your room and drop a roll of toilet paper in the middle of the floor.

Donna, in just a minute I will ask you to leave the room. While you are gone, one person in here will come unroll this roll of tissue and hide it somewhere on their person. It will be in their pockets, sleeves, socks, wherever. We will give them one minute to do it so they will need to hurry. They may be out of breath or sweaty or a little lumpy.

You may step outside now. When you come back in—if you can guess who has stuffed the tissue, you get this Happy Meal that has gotten incredibly cool since I bought it before coming here tonight, but there is a good toy this month.

The smell in the teen boys class is more than likely sour shoes. Death by fire is the only cure...for the shoes, not the teen boys.

47

Hallelujah Handshake

Have everyone stand up. Give a folded dollar bill to one student for every 7 you have in attendance. So if you have 32 students, how many would you give out? No, seriously I'm asking. Math is hard. Let's just say approximately $9.32. I'm kidding, obviously you'd give about 5 kids a folded dollar.

Have the students put the dollar in their right hand. When you say "go" everyone mills around shaking hands. As they shake people's hands they also say their name. If your students know one another well and really don't need to be refreshed on one another's names they can say an interesting fact about themselves or their favorite movie.

If you have the money in your hand, you have to pass it to next person when you shake their hand. You can't avoid people or keep the money in your other hand. They should try to keep the money as imperceptible as possible.

After a few minutes, yell "stop." Whoever has the money gets to keep it. Listen, 7 bucks is money well spent to find out that guy's name who has been coming for 2 years, and you call him "buddy," and it's too late for you ask him his name now.

If you want to really make it interesting, replace the dollar bill with a two dollar bill. They have them at the bank and they all look counterfeit.

Let's all stand. (Shake hands with however many people you have dollar bills for, passing the dollars as you shake.)

Walk around and shake hands with people. You have to say your name when you shake. Some of you have dollar bills in your hand now. When someone shakes your hand you have to pass the dollar off to them. NO KEEPING IT FOR YOURSELF!

Keep shaking until I say stop. You might even have to re-shake a few hands. If you have the money when I say stop, you get to keep the loot!

If I stop you in mid-handshake, the tie goes to the receiver.

Okay, shake it like a Polaroid picture.

Get a good, long, heavy rope and see if you can get the whole class to jump rope at once.

Cookie Face

This is a beautiful game that you can come back to from time to time. It's really funny the first time you see it. But amazingly, it's fun even after the initial "Ha Ha" moment because it becomes a skill game.

Bring two to five contestants to the front. Give them each an Oreo® cookie. Have a few extras on hand. Have the contestants twist the Oreo apart. Next, they lean their heads back and place the cookie with the white part facing down on their forehead.

When you say "Go" the contestants attempt to work the cookie into their mouths by contorting their face and slowly wriggle it to their mouths. They cannot use their hands. You will probably want to have the cameras ready for this.

If the cookie falls off, hand them another one and they jump right back in the game. Make sure you get one of your volunteers to play along on this one.

Say this

Hey, catch this. Catch this. Catch this. (That was you throwing an Oreo to three different people.)

Okay, you three step up here to the front of the room with your cookies. Untwist them for me. Take the part with gooey stuff on it, lean back and put it on your forehead.

When I say "Go," slowly work the cookie toward your mouth by wiggling your face. The first person to get their cookie in his or her mouth is the champ. If you drop your cookie we will get you another one (if it lands face down!) If you win, you get the other two people's cookies. I'm kidding, you get fame and riches. Ready? Go!

Like it or not, in our social media crazy age, many of our events are measured by their photo ops.

BFF

Sometime when you are talking about friendship, use this for a starter.

For this activity, you'll need four pieces of paper. Put a big "A" on two of them. Make a big "B" on the remaining two. Arrange two chairs back to back at the front of the room where you can see them from the side. Have two "friends" sit in the chairs. The reason I put "friend" in quotation marks is that you could have complete strangers play this if you'd like.

Give each friend an "A" paper and a "B" paper. They'll use these to answer questions. Tell them you will ask them a series of A or B questions, and they are to hold up the letter that goes with their answer.

The pair stays in the seats until their answers disagree. If they can get all ten the same, they are the champs.

It may be easier for the contestants if you tell one of them to answer the questions based on the actual way they feel, and for the other contestant to answer what he or she thinks the other person would say. This makes it a little more about skill and it's not solely just a game of matching opinions, but I really think matching opinions is more fun.

Here are some sample questions:

What would you rather do?

A. Shop   B. Go to a football game

Where would you rather eat?

A. A fast food joint   B. A fancy restaurant

What do you like best on a hot dog?

A. Mustard   B. Ketchup

Which is a better pet?
A. Cat   B. Dog

Which would you rather have bite you?
A. Snake   B. Spider

What would you rather do?
A. Read   B. Hike

Which do you like better?
A. Mars   B. Neptune

Which do you like better?
A. Beach   B. Mountains

Which is worse?
A. Splinter   B. Paper cut

Which do you prefer?
A. Coke   B. Pepsi

Say this

Are there two friends here tonight who have everything in common? Raise your hands if that is you.

You two come sit in these chairs. Hold these two signs that say "A" and "B."

I'm going to ask you a question that has "A" and "B" answers. Hold up your answer. As long as your answers match, you are in the game. When you disagree, you are out.

You can't talk. Here we go.

Hacky sacks are to sixteen-year-old boys what crossword puzzles are to my mom. It's also fun to use one of the cheap, plastic, lightweight, volleyballs and then get in a circle around a bucket and try to make it in the "basket" as a group.

Ultimate Frisbee

Most of the games in this book are inside, low impact games, so it might be nice to throw in an active game. And I know many of you are familiar with this gem, but stick with me. There are a couple of little twists that can make this brand new. If this is new to you, play it! This game is fun, high energy, unisexual, cheap, and takes almost no athletic ability.

You play this on the exact same field you would play flag football—end zones and all. Divide into two teams. I always tell people to find someone similar to them and stand by that person. Once everyone finds a buddy, have them go to opposite teams.

If you have a lot of students, you'll probably need something to help them know who is on their team. A cheap way to do this is to get some plastic ribbon, like a surveyor might use. It comes in bright colors. Get a different color for each team. Rip off pieces about 4-feet-long and give them to each team. Have them tie the ribbons around their heads and biceps or another visible spot.

These are the rules. The game starts by one team "kicking off" by throwing the frisbee to the other team and running down the field to defend their opponents. When your team has the frisbee, the goal is to move it to the goal line by passing it to your teammates. You can only take two steps while you are holding the frisbee. Like I said, you try to pass it to your teammates to move it down the field.

The other team tries to knock it down or intercept the frisbee. If it hits the ground the other team takes possession. Simple...and exhausting.

This is where the game gets fun. Sure, you can use a frisbee, but if you really want a party use a cabbage. (Buy a few spare ones.) If you really, really want a party use a squid instead of a frisbee. If you really, really, really want a party use a junior high guy's shoe. No, let's draw the line right before that.

Say this

Find somebody who looks like they have similar athletic ability to you. Unfortunately, Superman is a make-believe person so I will have Jake as my partner.

Good deal. Now one of you go to the pink ribbon team located beside this roll of pink ribbon, and one of you to the yellow ribbon team. Pink ribbon team, take this pink ribbon, rip off a piece, and tie it around you somewhere so we know whose team you're on. Yellow team, here is your yellow tape to do the same.

Yellow, you're going to throw it to the pink team to start the game. Pink, once you get the frisbee, you're trying to get it into the other team's end zone by throwing it to different members of your team. If you drop it or the other team intercepts the frisbee, they will start trying to score. Remember, you can't run with the frisbee. If you take more than two steps, the other team gets it.

I bet you can't lick your elbow.

51

Pantyhose Tug of War

You need a couple of pairs of pantyhose for this party. When buying pantyhose as a guy, trying to explain to the cashier that you are a student worker only makes you look creepier. The self-checkout is really your only hope to maintain dignity.

Take the pantyhose and tie them in a knot just below the crotch area. They're too weak in the crotch for this game, so you have to tie that area to give it strength. (That last sentence will come back to haunt me when it's taken out of context someday.)

Next, cut the toes off the ends. Get two people to pull the hose over their heads. It will be tough. You might even think they are too tight to fit. Keep stretching. Have the players pull the hose all the way down past their chins so they can hold the hose with their hands to keep them from pulling off.

Have the two players turn away from one another while holding the hose at the bottom of their faces, slowly pull away from one another. It's not so much about tug of war. It's more about making their faces look contorted. The hose will rip if the contestants pull hard enough.

Say this

Ryan and Lenea, come up here for a minute. We will have a little tug of war. Ropes are boring though, so we're using pantyhose.

You two pull the feet of these hose over your head. It's going to be tight, but you can do it. Hold them at your chin because it is time to tug.

Now, turn away from one another and start pulling in opposite directions. Don't pull too hard. We just want to see these beautiful faces. I think I'll snap a picture or two while you do this.

Use relay games sparingly. It's basically standing in line. I don't consider going to the post office and department of motor vehicles "fun times."

52

Winning Streak

In this game you will have everyone stand and pair up with someone. You will ask a question and give two possible responses. Students have to choose one in their heads. Say "3,2,1" then have the students say their answer out loud. If both partner's answers match, they stay together for the next round. If they don't match answers, they switch partners. They can find a new partner pretty quickly by putting their hands up when they need a new partner. It's not hard to have an even number of people. Have one of your leaders sit out if you need to.

Students keep up with the longest streak that they have with one partner. The longest winning streak wins. They are automatic new best friends.

Possible questions. Coke® or Pepsi®. Red or green. Snake or spider. Sperrys® or Chacos®. Kudzu or okra. French or Italian. Burrito or enchilada. Shooting star or double rainbow. Hamster or guinea pig. Car or truck. Baseball or football. Cat or dog. Steak or gold. Salt or pepper. Crickets or night crawlers. Superman or batman. Mexican or Chinese. You get the idea. They don't even necessarily have to make sense.

By the way, don't over-explain it. Kids will ask "Am I trying to match what he likes?" Leave it vague. Say, "You just want to say the same thing."

Everyone quickly get up and get a partner. Any time you don't have a partner in this game put your hand up to find someone available.

I'm going to give you two options. Pick one in your head. Then I'm going to say, "3, 2, 1" and I want you to call out one of the two options. If your answers match stay with that same partner. If they don't, find a new partner. Keep up with how many matches you get with a partner. Whoever has the most, has a new best friend. Remember to raise your hand when you need a new buddy.

Here we go. Chocolate or white milk? 3, 2, 1. Okay find a new partner quickly if you need one. Bacon or cookies. 3, 2, 1......

I have a joke about paper,
but I won't tell it. It's tearable.

Section 8

Help Beyond the Games

I realize this is a game book, but I want you to get your money's worth here. This section could be titled "Ramblings of a Gray Bearded Youth Pastor." These are just a few common problems I see in ministry that have almost done me in over the years.

Help! I Can't Get This Quiet Girl Engaged in Conversation.

I'm not a betting man, but I bet you have them. Picture this: Class has begun and you are dividing up for discussion time. You say, "This worked out great. We have an even number. Our groups work out perfectly. Oh…oops…sorry Jen, I didn't see you come in. You're so quiet you just kind of blended in with your chair there. You can just go…um, wherever." Jen, like human molasses, oozes toward a group. If the chairs are in a circle, her chair doesn't quite make it into the "O," which turns it into more of a "Q."

She seems satisfied there. The other kids don't mind her there. And you have run out of creative questions you have craftily tailored that you thought couldn't be answered with a shrug, although she has proven you wrong many times.

When this person was younger, it was enough to sit in silence. However, as these types of people get into middle school and high school, many times they will turn to fashion and music that is as far from mainstream as they can get. That is their goal—to stay out of the stream.

Many times these kids are highly intelligent. In some cases, this is what began their solitude. If they speak up they will be singled out for their intellect. I think we underestimate the power of their need to fit in. Even people that seem to work hard to stand out in the crowd with their clothes or tastes, will work hard to fit into the "stand out group," if that makes sense. But it's even more than that for the student we are talking about. She wants to disappear.

It seems to me that this girl says to herself, "I bet I am so in-significant that I can sit here and become nonexistent to this group." And we let it happen.

What can we do to engage these students?

Start the process with body language and a whisper. The best posture for a conversation with this student is shoulder to shoulder, not face to face. Even a face to face smile can feel threatening to this student.

Have a seat beside him or her (there is almost always a chair on either side available) and say, "I love it when you're here. You're important to our group." (This is true by the way.)

This a good start, however the problem is that this student is smart and will over-think your kindness and say, "The church had to pay him to say that." But it is the first step in this mar-athon.

The breakthrough will be made by that killer student you have. The student who is voted least likely to be a hypocrite will be the one to help the king or queen of solitude. Help your student leader realize that this is a process. By the way, if this "Michael Jordan of student leaders" is not coming to mind, you can give this a try.

Maybe tonight it's "Hey Jen, glad you're here!" And next week it's "Hey Jen, I'm trying to broaden my musical tastes. I trust your opinion. Who do you like?" Then the next week, "Wow Jen, I had to read those lyrics eight times to understand them, but it was cool. I have a seat I saved for you right here."

Think about how many times in the Bible we see Satan using loneliness in an attempt to defeat good people (1 Kings 19:10). Loners often fail. We need one another. These quiet students will run from God if we don't reach them.

The good news is this type of student becomes an incredible young adult. It seems like we don't see the effect on this person until they are in college. But more often than not they are smart, mature, and sincere in their young adult lives and they come to appreciate what you have done for them. By the way, this is what you've done for them: sincerely cared.

> **Chalkboard paint turns any wall into a prayer request/praise item bulletin board. Tape off a cool shape and knock it out.**

Help! I'm in a Slump.

It's important to keep in mind that it would be abnormal to live life in a never-ending state of bliss.

These low spots were felt by the greatest followers of Christ and even Christ Himself. Having the burden of ministering in a broken world *should* lead to periods of brokenness from time to time.

If you find yourself in a low place, welcome to the elite group that scientists refer to as *human*. Some of the symptoms of these slumps are feeling tired or washed out. You get a shorter fuse than usual around the people you care for most. Ministry can seem like a burden instead of the joy of your life. It's a general feeling of "Blah."

The bad news is—slumps will come. The good news is—they also go. There are a few things you can do to endure these low times:

- Go outside and read a book. (Sunshine is so good for us.)

- Try to write down exactly what you're experiencing. Include some things you'd recommend to someone going through a difficult time. It will help you now and possibly help others down the road.

- Give something away that will get you a smile in return. Buy some roses at the grocery store, and give them to the grandmotherly cashier who checks you out. Or ask on social media: "What is your favorite Sonic drink?" When people respond, show up at their door with their favorite drink.

- Read Lamentations chapter 3. That verse about teeth and gravel always gives me the heebie jeebies, but the hope of brand new mercy for today is worth it.

- Fast from something. Food works. Social media works even better sometimes. Replace those things with fellowship with your King.

> Unwrap two Starbursts. Give them to two students. Have them put the candy in their mouths without looking at the color. The first person who can tell you the color of their Starburst wins. They only get one try, so no guessing.

Help! I Want to Be a Better Mentor.

It is so easy to get overwhelmed by the task of discipling students and volunteers. There are one thousand kids at the high school up the road and thirty of them know you exist, but sometimes it feels like only about four of them like you. There is just so much to do. Where do you start?

Part of your ministry works like a flood light. You know how a flood light works. It shines a broad less intense glow over a wide area. Whenever you have an event or even a regular service with your students, you are using a flood light ministry. It's good to do that. You need to have these broad reaching times.

Mentoring is different. It is like a laser beam. Laser beams are intense pinpoints of light. In ministry, this is where you focus on one student or volunteer and really pour yourself into them.

Mentoring is front line discipleship. It is when you are trying to reproduce a better version of yourself. There is no shortcut to good mentorship. It takes time.

Once you identify a person you'd like to mentor, pray for them every day. It's important to have a couple of digital touches with them every week. Go a little deeper in your text than the normal "Praying for you" (although that is a good thing for them to know, too). A question that requires more than an emoji reply is a good way to go. Try, "How can I pray for you today?"

Encourage him or her with a text like, "Hey, read Acts 17:6. Man, maybe we can turn our town upside down. I hope you're leading folks today!"

Try to eat lunch or drink a slushie (sorry I don't like coffee) with them once a month. If you don't plan for it, it won't happen.

Give him (him, if you are a guy or her, if you are a girl) a few minutes at the beginning of one of your classes to do a devotion or talk about his favorite verse. The most valuable part of this exercise is the time you can spend with him leading up to it, when he shares with you and you lead him.

Mentor one student or one volunteer to start. Encourage that person to mentor someone.

I know it seems like a small thing to pour yourself into just one person, but remember Jesus had twelve and he *really* poured Himself into three of them. And you could make an argument that He had a special mentoring relationship with "the Beloved," John.

Help! I Can't Find Volunteers.

The health of your youth group will be concurrent to the health of your ministry volunteer helpers. You MUST find, challenge, and train your volunteer staff. If you happen to be the "Beatles" of student ministry and your ministry outgrows your volunteers, it will make you an old person prematurely.

The great thing is, these people need to help you just as badly as you need to be helped. Let's quickly discuss how to find them and train them.

Do not announce to everyone, "Hey, I need some volunteers to help with our student ministry." These dangerous words will repel the people you want and attract the people who are not ready to be volunteers.

Prayerfully go to individuals you trust and ask for their help. Tell them exactly what you want them to do. Don't assume they will figure it out. Actually, say the words, "I want you to play ping pong with at least one student before each of our meetings. Then sit with one of those guys in the service. Can you do that?"

I know that seems way too simple, but students are not used to people caring for them with no strings attached. Teaching volunteers to become student's cheerleaders can revolutionize their lives—students and leaders alike.

Handwritten notes of encouragement are worth more than cash money. Write them often!

Help! My Pastor Does Not Remind Me of Jesus.

This entry is not here to beat up senior pastors. Just like student ministers tend to get stereotyped as lazy, reckless, goofballs—senior pastors tend to be categorized as overbearing, ungrateful task masters who take credit for our hard work. Whoa! That just kind of effortlessly rolled off my tongue.

If your relationship with your pastor is strained, there are some things to remember as you navigate a tough time.

Try to focus on what you can control. You can't "fix" anyone, but yourself. Try to use your energy on maintaining your good attitude, and not on picking apart the attitude of someone beyond your control. This includes not downgrading or complaining to people in your church circle. It may be helpful to talk to someone totally removed from your situation, but complaining is really never the best use of your energy.

Take the high road. Do your best to be supportive and not divisive in any way. When all is said and done, you want to know you did everything you could to maintain peace and unity.

Be faithful to your work. Satan can use personalities to distract you from the work you have been called to. There is plenty of good work to keep you busy. You are serving Christ and His church.

Be submissive in matters where disagree with your pastor. Being submissive is strength, not weakness.

Faithfully pray for your pastor.

If it does get to the place where you need to move on, leave gently.

Please understand, you will survive this. With that in mind, let's make sure your character and integrity survive it as well.

> **No matter what the Internet says, frozen goldfish do not come back to life when thawed.**

Help! My Students Are in a Spiritual Struggle.

If you've been working with students for more than five minutes, you know what a wide spectrum of growth they represent. There are kids who have completely abandoned self and are serving God intently, and other types of students who were leaving a suicide note on the church office door for his girlfriend—and you invite him to stay for the service (true story). Don't you just love that?

Each has challenges. I want to focus just a minute on that student who is faithful and growing. He's dedicated and really trying to live for Christ.

This student is heading for a wall. I have seen this so many times. Shoot, I've seen it in *my* life. You come to this place of frustration because you are trying so hard to do the right thing and serve God, but it just feels like a constant struggle. It's like war. And in your mind you're thinking, *"Surely it's not supposed to be like this. I feel like all I do is fight and fail all the time. Maybe I'm just not cut out for this."*

It is so important to communicate to our students that **struggling is not losing.**

When Paul wrote to Timothy in 1 Timothy 6:12, he told him to "Fight the good fight of faith." He didn't say, "Chill the good chill" or "Relax the good relax." Living for the Lord feels like a fight sometimes.

Paul also told the Ephesians that they were in a wrestling match against evil forces (Eph. 6:12). Have you ever wrestled? It is the most exhausting, body punishing, frustrating thing you can do. And that's just putting on the leotard (or singlet for you wrestling purists)!

Seriously, find a way to encourage your warriors. They need to know that when it feels like a fight, they are doing something right. Encourage them to FIGHT!

Open two cartons of eggs and set the cartons on the floor. Take off your shoes and you can carefully stand with one foot on each.

Help! My Stomach Makes Noises in Church.

Scientists have proven that your stomach will not make noise unless it is the quietest most serious moment in a church service. What is up with this?

If you're shooting fireworks in a snare drum factory test hall: nothing. But anytime a dear saint is testifying and she takes a second to regroup because she is crying and the room is so quiet you can hear your shoestrings loosening, all of a sudden those three dozen pizza rolls you had for breakfast decide it's time for an encore appearance. And c'mon, let's be honest! That isn't a growl. We'll just call it the world's greatest untapped alternative fuel source.

Is there a worse noise on the planet? I was at a funeral the other day. I had enjoyed an order of fajitas for two before the service. I'm compelled to disclose that I was dining alone, which is probably the source of my problem.

Just as the lady stopped playing the organ, *my* organs took a turn. To my horror I felt the onset of the pressure, but I was not prepared for what happened next. My stomach actually called out a person's name. I couldn't make out the middle name but I did catch "Burt Blarnaby." And although I can't prove it, I'm pretty sure it said something in Latin last Tuesday. Hey! I don't even know Latin! Are my bowels actually taking online classes without my knowledge?

Listen, I know that I'm not the only victim. I've seen you squirm. No one is immune to this curse. But don't panic. I happen to be the world's leading authority on covering up this "phenomena."

Begin by sucking your stomach in, trying to touch your spine with your navel. For those special "Taco Bell" silent moments it may be necessary to karate chop yourself just below the ribcage while performing the aforementioned spinenavelostomy. And don't forget the vocal cover. Some use the cough, which is usually mistimed—only bringing attention to yourself and could even result in—well, a tragedy.

You may want to consider an "Amen" or possibly an agreeing grunt for cover. Dropping the hymnbook is risky (because of the pick-up), but effective. The most successful cover is still the mislead. Sit by me or whatever overweight person is handy and when the noise happens, quickly look at me disappointedly shaking your head. I'm a big boy, I'll take the blame and to be honest sometimes I'm not sure. It might be me!

Well, it's getting close to church time and this bucket of hummus ain't gonna eat itself. I hope this was helpful.

I love taping prizes to the bottoms of people's chairs.

What is **D6**?

BASED ON DEUTERONOMY 6:4-7

A **conference** for your entire **team**

A **curriculum** for every age at **church**

An **experience** for every person in your **home**

Connecting
CHURCH & HOME
These must work together!

D6 CONFERENCE
ONCE A YEAR

DEFINE & REFINE Your Discipleship Plan

www.d6family.com

ONE HOUR
A WEEK

POWER OF
PARENTAL INFLUENCE

A family-aligned curriculum
for every generation!

aligns all ages of the family

D6 CURRICULUM aligns small group environments at church so the entire family from kindergarten to grandparents, is studying the same theme at the same time. D6 helps parents and grandparents connect with kids and teens (even if they are miles away) through the use of devotional study guides, Splink, Home Connection, and other take-home resources that help equip the home.

D6 connects the church and home through generational discipleship.

www.d6family.com

BASED ON DEUTERONOMY 6:5-9

FREE SAMPLES AVAILABLE AT D6FAMILY.COM

CONNECTING WITH
YOUR TEENS

FROM RANDALL HOUSE

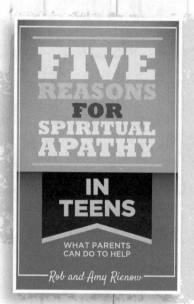

FIVE REASONS FOR SPIRITUAL APATHY IN TEENS

WHAT PARENTS CAN DO TO HELP

Rob and Amy Rienow

It's about pressing in to the heart of your teen, and pushing past the emotional struggle.

Price: **$9.99**
13-ISBN: 9780892659883

Parents and grandparents must express unconditional·love and give genuine attention to their teens cultivating faith and character for a lifetime.

HOW TO ORDER:
1-800-877-7030 OR
WWW.RANDALLHOUSE.COM

randall house

D6

WANT TO
CONNECT
WITH
TEENS
ON A
DEEPER
LEVEL?

TEACHING FOR
CHANGE

Eight Keys
for Transformational
Bible Study with Teens

KEN COLEY

D6FAMILY.COM

FOR PARENTS AND TEENS

S U R
V I V
I N G
CULTURE

When Character and Your World Collide

BY EDWARD E. MOODY

SURVIVING CULTURE
When Character and Your World Collide

Young people today are faced with many challenges that attempt to lure them away from the truth of Scripture and their foundation of faith. Dr. Moody shares strong advice with parents on the need to prepare young people to make wise decisions while navigating the culture of today.

Available at
d6family.com

PARENT EDITION

randall house
randallhouse.com
1-800-877-7030

d6family.com